A STUDENT HANDBOOK OF GREEK AND ENGLISH GRAMMAR

A STUDENT HANDBOOK OF GREEK AND ENGLISH GRAMMAR

ROBERT MONDI
and
PETER L. CORRIGAN

Hackett Publishing Company, Inc.
Indianapolis/Cambridge

Printed in the United States of America

16 15 14 13   1 2 3 4 5 6 7

For further information, please address
Hackett Publishing Company, Inc.
P.O. Box 44937
Indianapolis, Indiana 46244-0937

www.hackettpublishing.com

Cover design by Brian Rak
Interior design by Elizabeth L. Wilson
Composition by William Hartman

Library of Congress Cataloging-in-Publication Data
Mondi, Robert Joseph.
A student handbook of Greek and English grammar / Robert Mondi and Peter L. Corrigan.
pages cm
Includes index.
Text in English and Greek.
ISBN 978-1-62466-036-8 (pbk.) — ISBN 978-1-62466-037-5 (cloth)
1. English language—Textbooks for foreign speakers—Greek, Ancient. 2. English language—Foreign words and phrases—Greek, Ancient. 3. English language—Grammar, comparative and general—Greek, Ancient. 4. Greek language—Grammar, comparative and general—English. 5. Greek language—Foreign words and phrases—English. I. Corrigan, Peter L. II. Title.
PE1129.G7M66 2013
428.2'489—dc23   2013016425

The paper used in this publication meets the minimum requirements of American National Standard for Information Sciences—Permanence of Paper for Printed Library Materials, ANSI Z39.48–1984.

This book is dedicated to our wives,
Vicki (R.M.)
and
Junjuan (P.L.C.)

CONTENTS

I. PRELIMINARIES

II. THE SYNTAX OF NOUNS AND RELATED WORDS

III. THE SYNTAX OF VERBS AND RELATED ELEMENTS

IV. SOME OTHER GRAMMATICAL ELEMENTS

PREFACE

Primary language acquisition is one of the most miraculous achievements of the human organism. Within the first few years of life, and seemingly without conscious effort, children internalize one of the most complex mental structures they will ever learn. Furthermore, the degree to which children learn to speak "correctly" (i.e., according to the formal rules of grammar for the language being spoken) depends primarily on the correctness of the particular speakers they are imitating. So most children eventually learn not to say things like "more big" or "beautifuler," since few adults commit these grammatical errors. But if you were to ask not only children, but even most adults, what the "rule" is in English for adjectival comparison, the initial reaction would in most cases be hesitation and uncertainty. Those who eventually arrive at the correct formulation will generally do so by going through specific examples in their mind and deducing the rule empirically from what they just 'know' to be right or wrong.

All of which is to say that by the time it takes place (if it ever does), the formal study of the grammar of one's first language is largely descriptive rather than prescriptive—not learning *how* to say things, but rather *why* we say them as we do. By the time children are old enough to study the grammar of their own language, they already know how to speak it, and for the most part correctly, in accordance with rules that they perhaps cannot articulate but observe consistently. So what is the point of such study? True, it can help elucidate certain fine points of formally correct speech, ones that are rendered less transparent by the fact that so many speakers misapply them. So, for example, the student of grammar will learn why it is correct (at least grammatically, if not always contextually) to say things like "this is she," and to avoid the hypercorrect "between you and I." He or she may also learn how to avoid the common syntactic pitfall of non-agreement of subject and verb in sentences where they are widely separated. Do such sporadic benefits justify subjecting generations of school children to the comprehensive study of English grammar, as has been traditionally done?

Many modern educators have apparently answered this question in the negative. A minority of students entering college today will claim to have been taught formal grammar in high school, and the widespread ignorance of grammatical terms like "participle" or "gerund" substantiates their claim. Whether this negatively impacts their effective use of English is perhaps debatable; what is beyond debate is a severe loss on another front—the study of a foreign language, especially the classical languages. For here the learning is indeed prescriptive. Students must learn the rules governing how Romans and Greeks said things in order to translate what they said into English. And those rules are of necessity expressed in the abstract language of grammatical terminology. So those who earlier in their education escaped the grammatical study of English now pay the price: they must learn the principles of grammar in general at the same time that they are learning the grammar of Latin or Greek in particular. What makes this situation doubly unfortunate is that the traditional presentation of English grammar in the schools was heavily based on grammatical categories drawn from the classical languages. So the study of Latin and Greek by these earlier generations of students, already well versed in English grammar, was greatly facilitated by the fact that they were already familiar with precisely those grammatical terms and constructions that they would need for the study of the classical languages. Consequently, older textbooks took for granted this basic linguistic competence on the part of the student and focused exclusively on the grammar of Latin and Greek. These older textbooks are, needless to say, all but unusable in the modern American classroom.

This book is an attempt to remedy this situation for today's students of ancient Greek. Although most recent Greek textbooks do recognize that things have changed, and presume little or no previous linguistic experience on the part of the student, their remediation often amounts to little more than providing definitions of grammatical terminology. We present a fuller explanation and illustration of every grammatical entity, from the most basic to the most complex, first as it occurs in English and then in Greek. Our hope thereby is that the student will fully understand each item of grammar in and of itself, before seeing just how the Greek is or is not similar to the English. As a collateral benefit, the students will acquire a facility with the grammar of their own language, and come to know just why, for example, it is wrong to say "between you and I."

* * * * * * * *

We are pleased to acknowledge our gratitude to Dr. Emily B. West of St. Catherine University, who in her former capacity as Forum editor of *The Classical Journal* solicited beta-testers for an earlier iteration of this book; her interest in and support for this project were quite inspiring. The beta-testers themselves offered many suggestions and ameliorations for the text, and we remain most indebted to them. The anonymous readers retained by Hackett Publishing provided us with numerous comments which proved very helpful in preparing our final draft. Finally, it was a great pleasure for us to work with

Mr. Brian Rak of Hackett Publishing to bring this book to completion; Brian's input on key decisions proved invaluable, and we are most grateful to him for his patience and generosity.

* * * * * * * *

In an often-noted passage from his *Confessions*, Augustine lamented over the contrast between the sweetness and ease of primary language acquisition in the loving bosom of adoring relations, and the bitter labor of learning a foreign language (in his case, Greek) at the hands—and perhaps the whip—of his harsh tutors. Our hope is that use of this book can go some way toward mitigating that bitterness, even if it can't turn it completely into sweetness.

Robert Mondi

Peter L. Corrigan

January 2013

INTRODUCTION

REMARKS FOR INSTRUCTORS

Students enrolling in beginning courses in ancient Greek today bring with them the widest possible range of previous linguistic experience. Those who have studied Latin with some success are obviously in the best possible position, and much of the more basic material in this text will already be second nature to them. For those with experience in some other foreign language (especially a European language), at the very least such concepts as verb conjugation, noun gender, and noun-adjective agreement will be familiar. But even these fundamental ideas might be alien to the student approaching Attic Greek as a first foreign language (a less rare occurrence than one might think). Consequently, as regards syntax and morphology, English can fairly be said to be—among European languages at any rate—the worst starting point for the study of Latin or Greek. Confronted with this situation, we have opted to take the grammatical competence (or lack thereof) of this final group as our baseline and to define, explain, and illustrate even the most elementary terms and concepts, thinking that it is preferable for you to advise students to skip over what they already know rather than have to supplement what is here with further remedial explanations of your own.

We assume that this book will be used as a companion to whatever primary Greek textbook you are using in your course. In an ideal world, the topics in such an auxiliary resource would be arranged in the same order as they appear in the textbook. Since, however, there is such wide variety in the order of presentation in various beginning Greek textbooks commonly in use, this cannot be the case. Our decision was to present the material in the order traditionally employed in the reference grammars of the classical languages. This choice calls attention to the two-fold purpose that we envision this book can serve.

First and foremost, our intent is to introduce and/or reinforce the numerous grammatical concepts that your students will need in their study of ancient Greek. This is done by first defining and then illustrating in English—to the extent that this is possible—every such concept, from the most basic to the most advanced. To this end, the organizing principle of each chapter or section is, "English first." This is true of the book overall, in that the initial Preliminaries section draws solely on English to explain these most basic units of grammar, before any mention of Greek. Similarly, within each chapter dealing with a specific point of grammar, we first illustrate it with English examples and then go on to the Greek.

Our presentation might differ from some introductory texts in that the latter often present the many uses of a grammatical entity in a piecemeal fashion, spread over several chapters. The subjunctive mood, for example, or the dative case might be introduced along with one or two of the most common uses, with the other uses added sporadically in subsequent chapters. We here present all of the most important applications of a grammatical category at the time the category is introduced, thus enabling the student to get an overview of its syntactic range—a feeling for its linguistic logic, so to speak. Many of these uses will be revisited in subsequent chapters (cross references will point the way). So the use of the subjunctive in generalizing clauses will be noted when this verbal mood is first introduced, and then again later in the chapters on the various types of clauses that employ it. Consequently, we do not expect that you will cover the chapters of this book sequentially, as you would those of a primary textbook, but rather that you will call attention to the relevant sections where appropriate.

A second potential use we see for this text is as a reference work, filling the gap between the introductory text used in the beginning course and the standard reference grammars, such as those of Smyth or Goodwin. The latter offer far too much information for the beginning or intermediate student, even if they are available; but the former are often difficult to use as a reference tool, for precisely the reason noted above: material is organized for purposes of pedagogy, not reference. So the second-year student who perhaps wants to review the different uses of the dative case or the variety of Greek pronouns, will find them here conveniently gathered in one place, thus obviating the need to haul out the old introductory text and seek out all the places where these things are to be found separately (if they are there at all). You will quickly see that we have in places included more detailed information than the beginner will be able to digest, but the information will be of use to the more advanced student. This is particularly true of those sections we have set off in the text as Fine Points. Here too, we assume that you will direct the students' attention to the sections that are appropriate to each level of study.

We have included no exercises in the text. For the Greek, exercises will presumably be found in the textbook you are using. We do recommend that you on occasion create English exercises of your own to test the students' grasp, in their own language, of some of the topics that commonly present problems, such as relative clauses and participles, before turning to the Greek. You might, for example, give them pairs of short sentences and ask them to combine them into single sentences using active and passive participles, or relative clauses eschewing the universal "that" and requiring a choice of who, whom, which, or whose. Another useful and easily prepared exercise is to give students a page of English text (it can be anything) and ask them to do such things as underline all participles and indicate which noun they modify; indicate any subjunctive verbs that might appear; or state which case a given noun would be in if the passage were to be translated into Greek. Even if translation from English to Greek is not part of your pedagogical approach, this can be a beneficial activity.

REMARKS FOR STUDENTS

Trying to make sense out of language is a little like trying to catch sight of yourself blinking. The best tool for making sense of language is language itself, but when we use language, we tend to do so quite unselfconsciously. Language seems to come naturally to us. Like blinking.

For most Americans, at just about the time we're starting to feel pretty confident and competent with our first language, we're often thrown into a second. And if that second language is largely unspoken, like ancient Greek, we're asked to think fairly analytically about language in some unfamiliar ways. Ancient Greek is to native English what calculus is to arithmetic: most of the elements were there all along, but they're now applied in some striking and novel manners.

And like calculus again, beginning Greek isn't easy. That simple truth cannot be whitewashed. Some foreign languages (like Latin, for example) are hardest at the intermediate level, but ancient Greek is hardest at the beginning. It is the intent of this book to make learning Greek easier for you by comparing it most closely to the language you already know: English. By understanding this comparison better, you can free up your brain to do more of the mechanical tasks of learning Greek vocabulary and morphology (endings).

Though it may seem otherwise, the study of grammar is actually glamorous. If you look up the words "grammar" and "glamour" in an etymological dictionary, you'll discover that they are both derived from the same Greek word meaning "letter." You'll also notice a definition for the former that reads something like this: that field of linguistic study which pertains to a language's inflectional forms or other means of specifying the relations of words within the phrase, clause, or sentence, and with the rules for using these in conformity with standard or established usage. So wear your new-found learning like the fine and stylish look that it is!

This is what we think is the best and most productive procedure for using this book. When you are assigned to read a section of this book, concentrate first on English usage. Make sure you clearly understand how the English works within the assigned section. Only after you've secured that understanding should you analyze how the corresponding Greek works. At that point you can make special note of both the commonalities and the differences—now you're achieving a basic competency. But the next step brings you to true proficiency: grasping the fine points of a language. We will provide you with sufficient basics and fine points in this book to sophisticate your knowledge of both Attic Greek and English.

A second valuable use for this volume is in ongoing review and recovery—a process you should be continually engaged in. The more times you review grammatical concepts the firmer they'll be fixed in your active comprehension. So peruse this book often; and those sections containing more difficult concepts you should peruse even more often.

This book is only one part of an essential learning troika for you. The second part is your instructor, who will clarify any uncertainties for you and provide other examples to reinforce our basic observations. If something you read here really piques your curiosity, your instructor can assist you with reference works which allow you to plumb deeper. The third part of the troika is your main Greek text, which this volume is only meant to supplement. Your main text supplies all foreground, while this book offers only background. The two books together can provide you with all the information you need, so that with every new point of Greek grammar you can confidently claim, "Ah-ha! I really get it now."

As a supplement not only to your elementary Greek textbook, this volume can also be used later in conjunction with your intermediate text and your first advanced texts. Indeed, this book can serve you until you're at home with the more comprehensive grammars cited below. The point is: consult this book whenever you're exposed to a linguistic concept or a technical term that baffles you in English as much as in Greek. By having the familiar explained to you, the foreign should seem much less foreign. And in the long run, your love and admiration for ancient Greek will only increase as you recognize it for a far more straightforward historical and cultural artifact than the language you happen to speak.

SUGGESTIONS FOR FURTHER READING

The most accessible modern grammars of English are:

Aarts, Bas, *Oxford Modern English Grammar.* Oxford University Press, Oxford and New York, 2011.

Huddleston, Rodney, and Geoffrey K. Pullum, *The Cambridge Grammar of the English Language.* Cambridge University Press, Cambridge and New York, 2002.

A fun and fascinating read can be found with this classic:

Fowler, W. H., *A Dictionary of Modern English Usage* (3rd edition revised by R. W. Burchfield). Oxford University Press, Oxford and New York, 2004 (first published 1906).

For a good historical overview of Greek, see:

Palmer, Leonard Robert, *The Greek Language.* University of Oklahoma Press, Norman, 1996 (reprinted from 1980).

If you're interested in how ancient Greek was probably spoken, you can refer to:

Allen, W. Sidney, *Vox Graeca: The Pronunciation of Classical Greek* (3rd edition). Cambridge University Press, Cambridge and New York, 1987 (first published 1968).

Of all intermediate Greek grammars, the best known are:

Goodwin, William W., *A Greek Grammar* (revised by Charles Burton Gulick), Ginn and Company. Boston, 1930 (first published 1879).

Hadley, James, *A Greek Grammar for Schools and Colleges* (revised by Frederic De Forest Allen). American Book Company, New York, 1884 (first published 1860).

Morwood, James, *Oxford Grammar of Classical Greek.* Oxford University Press, Oxford and New York, 2003.

Pratt, Louise H., *The Essentials of Greek Grammar: A Reference for Intermediate Readers of Attic Greek.* University of Oklahoma Press, Norman, 2010.

To date, the only advanced grammar of Greek in English is:

Smyth, Herbert Weir, *A Greek Grammar for Colleges* (revised by Gordon M. Messing). Harvard University Press, Cambridge, MA, 1956 (first published 1918).

Most or all of these books can be found in your college's or university's library.

I. PRELIMINARIES

1. INFLECTION

In American English, "inflection" usually refers to the tone with which a word or phrase is uttered.

But in Greek (and many other languages), **inflection** refers to the affixes added to word-roots (of nouns, verbs, adjectives, and pronouns) to specify their function within a sentence, clause, or phrase. An **affix** is any semantically meaningful element added to a word-root:

The person reads the indictment.

Father's horses helped them.

I had competed very proudly.

ὁ ἄνθρωπος ἀναγιγνώσκει τὴν γραφίαν.

οἱ τοῦ πατρὸς ἵπποι τούτοις ἐβοήθουν.

ἠγωνίσμην εὐπρεπέστατα.

Thus, we meet a very important axiom for translating Greek: *function follows form*. That is, the form (also called the **morphology**) a Greek word takes with respect to its inflection(s) points to its specific grammatical function. Therefore, the more thoroughly you learn the inflections of Greek, the better you'll be enabled to translate.

Suffixes (affixes added to the end of a word-root) and **prefixes** (affixes added to the beginning of a word-root) constitute the standard affixes in English:

unsupported

In addition to these, Greek also employs **infixes** (i.e., inflectional elements of significance placed within words):

παυσόμεθα: we will stop

Far and away, though, suffixes represent the most common and most important inflectional element of Greek word formation.[1]

Greek's reliance on inflection to indicate grammatical function carries a consequence that's sometimes hard to adjust to, especially at first: typically, Greek isn't read strictly from left to right, as English is. Therefore, try to get into the habit of reading not word by word and left to right but by properly identifying the inflections on words and by isolating semantically linked phrases and clauses.

Some older grammar books occasionally refer to morphology and inflectional endings as **accidence**.

1. For non-standard English, consider the word "unfreakingbelievable," which exhibits a prefix (un-), an infix (-freaking-), and a suffix (-able).

2. PARTS OF SPEECH

2.1 NOUNS

A **noun** is a word that refers to a person, place, concrete object, or abstract idea. If it refers to only one such entity, it is a **singular noun**, if more than one, a **plural noun**:

> The shepherd guards his flocks on the mountainside.
>
> Philosophy teaches us to live the good life.

If the noun is the name of someone or something, it is a **proper noun**:

> Pericles was a democratic leader in Athens.

If not, it is a **common noun**:

> Pericles was a democratic leader in the city.

A noun used as a **complement** (that is, as a word needed to complete the sense of another word or phrase) after a linking verb (see §2.6 below) is called a **predicate noun**:

> Socrates was a critic of the Sophists.
>
> Socrates remains an inspiration for those in search for the truth.

Some grammar books use the word **substantive** to designate a noun or any other part of speech (e.g., an adjective or verb) used as a noun.

2.2 ADJECTIVES

An **adjective** is a word that characterizes or describes a noun:

> The angry Greeks launched many ships to rescue the abducted queen.
>
> Safe at last, the sailors made an offering to the gods.
>
> Panting, the messenger reported that the Persians had been defeated at Marathon.

Sometimes the adjective may appear after linking verbs, in which case it is called a **predicate adjective**:

This orator is eloquent.

The children seem happy.

I became angry.

Demonstrative adjectives express the relative closeness of a noun to the speaker:

These verses are inferior to those poems written by the ancient poets.

That army will never conquer this city.

2.3 ARTICLES

When used with a noun, the **definite article** marks the noun as specific or unique:

The king of Persia led his army against the Greeks.

Socrates was the philosopher who spoke the truth.

The **indefinite article** marks the noun as merely a member of a class or category:

A king of Persia is someone to be feared.

Socrates was a philosopher who spoke the truth.

2.4 PRONOUNS

A pronoun is a word used in place of a noun. **Personal pronouns** are employed when both speaker and listener presumably know who is being referred to. In the case of a **1st person pronoun** ("I"/"we"), the referent is (or includes) the speaker, and in that of a **2nd person pronoun** ("you"), it is (or includes) the listener:

I can see you, but you can't see me.

We learn truth through suffering.

Third person pronouns refer to things or persons other than the speaker or listener, and their referents are therefore not self-evident. They generally refer to something or someone mentioned previously, and thus eliminate the need for repetition:

> The Athenians listened to the Spartan herald, but they did not believe him.
>
> I read that book, but I did not understand it.

Interrogative pronouns are used in questions, which can be either direct or indirect:

> Who is making that noise?
>
> I know what you did.

Indefinite pronouns imply an ignorance of their precise referent:

> Someone is sneaking through the gate.
>
> I know you are hiding something from me.

Relative pronouns introduce clauses that characterize a noun or pronoun located elsewhere in the sentence:

> We can't trust a man who talks of peace but prepares for war.
>
> He whom the gods love dies young.

2.5 PREPOSITIONS

A **preposition** is a word used in a phrase with a noun (or other substantive) expressing that noun's relationship to another word or idea:

> Few citizens came to the assembly.
> (prepositional phrase: "to the assembly")
>
> We sat in the theater all day.
> (prepositional phrase: "in the theater")
>
> Antigone was praised by the philosophers.
> (prepositional phrase: "by the philosophers")

Alcibiades left with them.
(prepositional phrase: "with them")

2.6 VERBS

The word that expresses the acting, being, doing, or the like, connecting the subject to the predicate in a clause or sentence, is called a **verb**:

Odysseus wandered for ten years.

Pericles is our leader.

Verbs that do not express a particular action but describe or define the subject are called **linking verbs**:

Pericles is our leader.

The athletes seem tired.

Sophocles has become quite old.

In English, a verb can be accompanied by one or more **auxiliary verbs**:

Hera will be honored by this. (The verb "honor" here is augmented by the auxiliary verbs "will" and "be.")

2.7 PARTICLES

A **particle** is a word (or pseudo-word, so to speak) added to convey earnestness, hesitation, uncertainty, doubt, or equivocation. While it is possible for particles to be omitted grammatically, semantically they add tone, coloration, and nuance, especially in rhetorical as well as conversational settings:

That woman is a, er, friend of mine.

Um, let me think about that for a moment.

It's a beautiful statue, eh?

Ah, those were the days!

The answer to that question, well, we may never know.

It's about, hmm, three miles from here.

2.8 CONJUNCTIONS

A word that links two or more grammatically equivalent parts is a **conjunction**:

Plato and Xenophon were his students.
(linking nouns)

Tomorrow, they will fight or withdraw.
(linking verbs)

Lycurgus was severe but just.
(linking adjectives)

The Athenians will resist if the Persians attack.
(linking clauses)

2.9 INTERJECTIONS

An **interjection** is a word or phrase said in exclamation, independent from its grammatical or syntactic context:

My wife—alas!—is dead.

Damn! I lost that bet.

O Poseidon! What rotten luck!

2.10 ADVERBS

We traditionally define an **adverb** as a word that can modify a verb, an adjective, or another adverb:

Pericles was very persuasive.
(modifying an adjective)

He spoke very clearly.
(modifying another adverb)

We eagerly listened to him.
(modifying a verb)

Generally, English adverbs express temporal (i.e., pertaining to time) or locative (i.e., pertaining to location) relations, manner, or degree.

3. SENTENCES, CLAUSES, PHRASES

3.1 SENTENCES

In practice, the parts of speech discussed in §2 are combined to produce sentences. A **sentence** is a unit of speech that is syntactically self-contained, consisting minimally of a **subject** (stated or implied), usually a noun or a pronoun telling what the topic of the sentence is, and a **predicate**, which says something about the subject and (in English) must at the very least contain a verb:

> Plato was a student of Socrates.
>
> None of the students of Socrates thought that he was justly condemned.

In the first sentence, "Plato" is the subject, and "was a student of Socrates" is the predicate. In the second, "None of the students of Socrates" forms the subject, and "thought that he was justly condemned" is the predicate.

3.2 CLAUSES

Like a sentence, a **clause** also has a subject and predicate but may not express a complete thought. If a sentence contains more than one clause, the clauses are generally linked by conjunctions. Clauses that would be capable of standing by themselves as complete sentences are called **independent**; those that would not are called **dependent** or **subordinate**. The incompleteness of a subordinate clause is often the result of an initial **subordinating conjunction** (see §28):

> Since Plato was a student of Socrates . . .
>
> If none of the students of Socrates thought that he was justly condemned . . .

An independent clause, also referred to as the **main clause,** is needed to complete the sentence:

> Since Plato was a student of Socrates, he greatly mourned his death.
>
> If none of the students of Socrates thought that he was justly condemned, why didn't they help him escape?

A sentence consisting of only a main clause is called a **simple sentence**; a sentence consisting of a main clause and one or more subordinate clauses is called a **complex sentence**. A **compound sentence** is one containing two or more independent clauses linked with a **coordinating conjunction** (see §28).

If the subordinate clause itself contains a subordinate clause, the two parts of that clause are designated the **principal clause** and the **dependent clause**.

> I wondered why, if Socrates had so many students, they didn't help him escape.

In this sentence, the principal clause is "why they didn't help him escape," and the dependent clause is "if Socrates had so many students."

3.3 PHRASES

A **phrase** is a group of words that forms a grammatical unit but lacks a subject or a predicate or both. There are various types of phrases:

> **Noun phrase**: The victorious athlete was greeted as a hero.
>
> **Verb phrase**: The victorious athlete was greeted as a hero.
>
> **Adjectival phrase:** Angry at the insult, Alcibiades left the party.
>
> **Prepositional phrase**: With hard work, you will succeed in the course of time.
>
> **Participial phrase**: Hastening to the city, he warned the citizens of the imminent attack.
>
> Attacked by the barbarians, the Greeks showed great valor.
>
> **Infinitive phrase**: Do you want to join the feast?
>
> **Absolute phrase**: Things being what they are, this is the best we can do.

The arrangement of words (with their appropriate morphology) according to their proper usage into semantically meaningful sentences, clauses, and phrases is commonly referred to as **syntax**.

II. THE SYNTAX OF NOUNS AND RELATED WORDS

4. NOUNS

As defined above (§2.1), a noun is a word that refers to a person, place, concrete object, or abstract idea. In Greek, each standard noun has three inherent characteristics: case, number, and gender. As case tends to be the most complicated of these three characteristics, we will discuss it last.

4.1 NUMBER

Number is a fairly straightforward notion in English, because English has only two numbers: **singular** (denoting one) and **plural** (denoting more than one):

The horseman is safe.

The horsemen are safe.

English plurals are most commonly created with the addition of the inflection *-(e)s*:

tale → tales

box → boxes

Sometimes a plural in English involves a vowel change:

goose → geese

mouse → mice

Sometimes plurals involve a consonant change:

knife → knives

And sometimes there is no change in plurals:

one sheep → two sheep

one deer → two deer

Rarely, plurals exhibit the ancient Germanic plural inflection:

child → children

ox → oxen[1]

Also rare are the rather subtle distinctions English can make with plurals:

six fish = fish all of the same species

six fishes = fishes of varied species

Some **collective nouns** (nouns that denote a collection of objects, ideas, or creatures), though singular in inflection, are typically construed as grammatical plurals:

The people are satisfied.

The cattle were fed.

Note, however, that these collective nouns can sometimes be pluralized (cf. fishes, above):

The peoples of the world are satisfied.

As with English, Greek nouns are typically singular or plural:

ὁ ἱππότης ἐστὶ σόος.
    The horseman is safe.

οἱ ἱππόται εἰσὶ σόοι.
    The horsemen are safe.

The change in number is signified by changes in the inflections.

Though rather rare, a third number, the **dual**, was inherited from Greek's parent-language (Indo-European) to refer to things that commonly occur in pairs (e.g., eyes, ears, hands, feet, parents, twins, close friends):

---

1. But be careful—chicken is not the plural of chick!

τὼ ὀφθαλμώ: the (two) eyes

τὼ χρυσὰ χεῖρε: the (two) golden hands

The dual number ceases to be used in Greek literature by the end of the fourth century BCE.[2]

4.2 GENDER

Though they are not much in evidence, English has three grammatical genders: **masculine**, **feminine**, and **neuter**. Generally, these genders are determined by biology; that is, things biologically male are grammatically masculine, things biologically female are grammatically feminine, and things which have indeterminate or no biological gender are grammatically neuter. Sometimes, when certain genderless things (such as ships or polities or institutions) are referred to in highly romanticized or emotionalized rhetoric, they are found in the feminine gender:

The law is a demanding mistress.

The *Andrea Doria* went down with most of her crew.

Harvard College welcomed me into her warm embrace.

Representations of things biologically gendered can frequently employ either the corresponding gender or a neuter:

Shakespeare's Iago is perfect: he is the very picture of evil.

Shakespeare's Iago is perfect: it is the very picture of evil.

This Minnie Mouse is different; her bow is on the left side.

This Minnie Mouse is different; its bow is on the left side.

2. Though lacking an actual dual number, English sometimes displays grammatical uncertainty over duals. For example, do you say, "A pair of corduroys is hanging in my closet" or "A pair of corduroys are hanging in my closet"? Similarly, which is correct: "Last spring, a couple of robins was nesting on our porch" or "Last spring, a couple of robins were nesting on our porch"?

English used to employ the masculine gender as its so-called **dominant gender** for grammar, that is, as the default grammatical gender when the biological gender of a noun or pronoun was indeterminate:

Anyone [even if the person is female] who says this should check his facts.

Amidst considerable confusion (not to mention dubious grammar), English now commonly pluralizes personal pronouns precisely because they are gender-indeterminate:

Anyone who says this should check their facts.

Attic Greek also has the three grammatical genders of masculine, feminine, and neuter. In Greek, however, grammatical gender is not simply determined by biological gender; often the gender of a Greek noun is seemingly arbitrary or influenced by the gender of other nouns that it in some way resembles. In fine, apart from the names of people (who are understood as being either feminine or masculine), all other Greek nouns have a grammatical gender which is often unpredictable (and must, therefore, be learned when the noun is first introduced in vocabulary).

Greek also has the notion of dominant gender. For nouns of mixed or indeterminate gender, the masculine gender is commonly applied:

οἱ Πέρσαι εἰσί βαρβαρικοί: The Persians [males and females] are barbaric.

καὶ δ' αἱ γυναῖκες καὶ οἱ ἄνδρες ἦσαν μεγάλοι: Both the women and the men were large.

If compound abstract nouns are used in the Greek subject, often the predicate is neuter plural:

τὸ θάρσος καὶ ἡ τόλμα καὶ ὁ νοῦς εἰσι χρήσιμα: Courage, daring, and intelligence are useful [things].

4.3 CASE

Indo-European, the common ancestor of Greek and English, had many different noun cases. Each case expressed a specific noun function within sentences, clauses, and phrases and was distinguished by its own proper inflections. Such functions included direct object, instrumentality, possession, subject, location, and the like.

English nouns don't really preserve the feature of case and noun function, unless one considers the use of *-'s* and *-s'* to express possession:

the book's binding

the kittens' mother

Besides the possessive case, the subjective case and the objective case are also grammatically observed in English even though they're not inflectionally observed in nouns. For case inflections in English, one must look to some pronouns (see §8).

Greek preserved five of Indo-European's main noun cases and functions, and they are identified by means of inflectional endings:

4.3.1 Nominative case: the sentence's or clause's subject and predicate subject

ὁ Περικλῆς ἐστι στρατηγός: Pericles is general.

4.3.2 Genitive case: Many of the uses of the genitive case in Greek can be rendered in English with the preposition "of":

Possession: ἡ θυγάτηρ τοῦ Πινδάρου: the daughter of Pindar, Pindar's daughter

Source or material: τὸ δόρυ τῆς μελίας: the spear of ash wood

Descriptive quality: ἄνθρωπός τις τῶν ἔργων: a person of deeds

Part of a whole: τὸ μέγιστον μέρος τοῦ δήμου: the largest part of the people

οἱ ἀνδρειότατοι τῶν Ἀθηναίων: the bravest of the Athenians

When used in conjunction with a noun that carries a verbal sense, the genitive can function as either the subject or the object of the action implied by the noun and is designated as either the **subjective genitive** or the **objective genitive**, respectively:

ἆρα οὐκ αἰσθάνῃ τὸν φόβον τῶν πολεμίων;

Do you not perceive the fear of the enemy? (I.e., the enemy's fear of us: the enemy is here the subject of the idea of fearing.)

φόβος τῶν πολεμίων ἐκώλυσεν ἡμᾶς μένειν.

Fear of the enemy prevented us from remaining. (I.e., our fear of the enemy: the enemy is the object of the idea of fearing)

4.3.3 Dative case: indirect object; instrumentality; agency in the passive perfective system of verbs; possessor of nominative objects when used with the verb *to be;* other uses, as well (see §5 below):

λέγε τοῖς δούλοις ταῦτα: Tell (to) the slaves these things.

ἔβαλε με λίθῳ: He hit me with a stone.

ταῦτα πέπρακται τῇ ἐκκλησίᾳ: These things have been done by the assembly.

πατρὶ τρεῖς ἡμίονοί εἰσιν: Father has three mules [literally: there are to father three mules].

4.3.4 Accusative case: the direct object of verbs and deverbatives (see §11.2); the subject of an infinitive when different from subject of the main verb (see §16.2); other uses, as well (see §5):

ὁ Σωκράτης Ἀσπασίαν ἠσπάζετο: Socrates was greeting Aspasia.

νικᾶν τοὺς Ἀθηναίους φημί: I say that the Athenians are winning.

προσαγορεύων τὴν βούλην, ὁ Ἀριστείδης εἶπεν: Addressing the council, Aristides spoke.

The genitive, dative, and accusative cases are collectively referred to as the **oblique cases**.

4.3.5 Vocative case: direct address and **apostrophe** (a sudden exclamatory address to a person or thing that may not even be present or real):

ὦ Ζεῦ: O Zeus!

ἔστιν, ὦ γρᾶες, στρατηγός τις: There is, old women, a general.

ὦ ἐλπί: O hope!

In English, because nouns don't exhibit the case differentiation (except in the possessive), they don't behave according to much of a system of inflectional endings (**paradigm**). In Greek, each noun generally conforms and belongs to one of three consistent patterns or paradigms of inflection, called **declensions**. In the 1st declension, the vowels -α- and -η- predominate in the inflections. In the 2nd declension, -ο- predominates in the case inflections. And in the 3rd declension, -ι-, -ε-, -υ-, and certain diphthongs predominate. If you learn the 1st and 2nd declensions thoroughly, the somewhat more difficult 3rd declension becomes relatively easier to master.

5. SPECIAL USES FOR NOUN CASES

Greek has some subtle and unique ways of expressing common ideas by means of nouns and noun phrases. The array of Greek noun cases affords the ability to make meaningful and sometimes fascinating distinctions. The locutions we survey in this chapter range from the fairly idiomatic to the highly rhetorical.

5.1 PERSONAL AGENCY

In passive constructions (see §11.5), where the action of the verb and the subject acted upon are usually the emphasis of the sentence, clause, or phrase, it is sometimes necessary also to specify the person by whom the passive action was done. In English, we do this by using the preposition "by":

The letters were brought by slaves.

This same idea is also most often expressed by a preposition in Greek: ὑπό with the genitive case. But this construction is most commonly employed when the passive verb (or deverbative; see §11.2) is in the present, imperfect, future, or aorist tense. When the verb is in the perfect, pluperfect, or future perfect tense or when a passive verbal (see §15) is found, personal agency is expressed with a simple dative, without a preposition:

The letters were brought by slaves.
αἱ ἐπιστολαὶ ἠνέχθησαν ὑπὸ τῶν δούλων.

The letters have been brought by slaves.
αἱ ἐπιστολαὶ ἐνηνεγμέναι εἰσί τοῖς δούλοις.

The letters must be brought by slaves.
αἱ ἐπιστολαὶ οἰστέαι εἰσί τοῖς δούλοις.

5.2 EXCLAMATION

When we're angry, surprised, frightened, or otherwise agitated, we tend to blurt things out without much regard for the grammar or syntax of our native language. Typically, however, we don't employ utter gibberish to respond to such conditions.

In a Greek exclamation involving a direct address, the vocative case (or, more rarely, the nominative case) is used. If respect or politeness is being expressed, the interjection ὦ precedes the noun.

ὦ Ζεῦ: O Zeus!

οὗτος, τί πράττεις;: You here, what are you doing?

When the interjections φεῦ or οἴμοι, "alas," are used, the nominative case follows if the exclamation is 1st person; the genitive case follows if the exclamation is 2nd or 3rd person. If neither interjection is used and the exclamation is 3rd person, a genitive is typically employed:

οἴμοι τάλαινα: alas for miserable me!

φεῦ τῶν ἀνδρῶν: alas for the men!

τῆς ἀδικίας: O the injustice!

In exclamations that express oaths or swearing, the noun is placed in the accusative case preceded by the adverbs νή or ναὶ μά, if the oath is positive; or μά or οὐ μά, if the oath is negative:

ναὶ μὰ Δία: yes, by Zeus!

μὰ Ἑρμῆν: no, by Hermes!

5.3 MEANS/MANNER

In noun phrases that answer the question "how?," a variety of expressions can be found. For an actual instrument or physical object, the simple dative case is used in Greek. If the means or manner is abstract, a simple dative is usually employed when the noun is modified by an adjective; if no modifier is present, the prepositions σύν (with the dative noun) or μετά (with the genitive noun) are used.

We will do this with stones.
τοῦτο ποιήσομεν λίθοις.

We will do this with much eagerness.
τοῦτο ποιήσομεν πολλῇ σπουδῇ.

We will do this with eagerness.
τοῦτο ποιήσομεν μετὰ σπουδῆς/σὺν σπουδῇ.

Some simple nouns in either the dative or accusative case take on an almost adverbial force. These expressions, while relatively few in number, are quite high in frequency.

πρόφασιν: allegedly

προῖκα: for free

κόσμῳ: in order, properly

βίᾳ: by force, forcefully

ἰδίᾳ: privately

δίκῃ: justly

Occasionally the expression can be found with a definite article or an indefinite or interrogative adjective.

τρόπον τινά: in some way

τίνα τρόπον: in what way?

τῇ ἀληθείᾳ: in truth

τῷ λόγῳ: in theory, in principle

τῷ ἔργῳ: in fact

τῷ ὄντι: in reality

5.4 PRICE/VALUE

Greek has one common way to express the cost at which objects are bought, sold, or valued. Two alternative expressions can also be found. The simple genitive case has the highest frequency in this context; e.g.,

I will work for ten minae.
ἐργάσομαι δέκα μνῶν.

Sometimes the preposition ἀντί with the genitive case is used.

I will work in return/exchange for ten minae.
ἐργάσομαι ἀντὶ δέκα μνῶν.

A dative of means (see above) can also be used in this setting; e.g.,

I will work at [the price of] ten minae.
ἐργάσομαι δέκα μναῖς.

When something (or someone) is being appraised or valued, the worth is usually expressed with the preposition περί plus the genitive or, rarely, in the genitive without the preposition.

a house worth much (money)
οἰκία περὶ πολλοῦ (χρήματος)

horses of little value
ἵπποι (περὶ) ὀλίγου

5.5 TIME EXPRESSIONS

Most expressions of time in English employ prepositional phrases.

He hid in the forest for three days.

We will see you on Saturday.

The job will be done in September.

The play starts at eight o'clock.

I will call you within a week.

In Greek, it is commonly a noun or noun phrase alone that expresses an interval or point in time, without prepositions. All three oblique cases may be so used.

To specify the time at which something takes place, the dative case is employed.

ὁ ἄγγελος ἀφίκετο τῇ τρίτῃ ἡμέρᾳ.
The messenger arrived on the third day.

To indicate the duration of an event or action, the accusative case is employed.

αἱ στρατιαὶ ἐμάχοντο τρεῖς ἡμέρας.
The armies were fighting for three days.

The genitive case indicates the <u>time within which</u> something takes place.

τοὺς πολεμίους νικήσομεν τριῶν ἡμερῶν.
We will defeat the enemy within three days.

5.6 COMPARISON

English employs the conjunction "than" to introduce the second element of a comparison.

The teacher is wiser than the student.

In the event that this element is a personal pronoun, where English still preserves case distinctions, it properly must be in the same case as the item to which it is being compared:

My brother is taller than <u>I</u>.

People love my brother more than <u>me</u> [i.e., more than they love me].

My brother's house is bigger than <u>mine</u>.

Greek syntax provides two ways of expressing such comparisons. One is precisely the same as the English construction, using the Greek conjunction ἤ.

ὁ διδάσκαλος σοφώτερος ἢ ὁ μαθητής.
The teacher is wiser than the student.

τῷ διδασκάλῳ πιστεύομεν μᾶλλον ἢ τῷ μαθητῇ.
We trust the teacher more than [we trust] the student.

τῷ διδασκάλῳ πιστεύομεν μᾶλλον ἢ ὁ μαθητής.
We trust the teacher more than the student [trusts the teacher].

Since all nouns in Greek show case distinction, the noun following the conjunction will be in the same case as the item it is being compared to. One result of this is that the Greek comparison will lack the ambiguity that might be present in the English, as the second and third examples illustrate.

The other option in Greek is to eliminate the conjunction ἤ and put the noun that would follow it into the genitive case.

ὁ διδάσκαλος σοφώτερος τοῦ μαθητοῦ.

τῷ διδασκάλῳ πιστεύομεν μᾶλλον τοῦ μαθητοῦ.

This option, it should be noted, can introduce the same ambiguity into the Greek comparison as is present in the English.

In order to express the **degree of difference** involved in the comparison, a word expressing quantity or extent can be placed in the dative case:

ὁ διδάσκαλος ὀλίγῳ σοφώτερος τοῦ μαθητοῦ.

The teacher is a little wiser than the student.

τῷ διδασκάλῳ πιστεύομεν πολλῷ μᾶλλον τοῦ μαθητοῦ.

We trust the teacher much more than the student.

Finally, in expressions involving the superlative degree of the adjective, the genitive case is used to denote the class that constitutes the basis of comparison:

ὁ Σωκράτης σοφώτατος ἦν τῶν Ἀθηναίων.

Socrates was the wisest of the Athenians.

6. ADJECTIVES

An adjective is a word that characterizes or describes a noun. In English, adjectives are most commonly placed directly before the noun that they modify and after the article, if there is one.

The wise father praises a good son.

Exceptions to this rule include poetic expressions (e.g., "Once upon a midnight dreary"); certain common adjectival phrases derived from French (e.g., "a court martial," "an heir apparent," "an attorney general"); intensive adjectives (e.g., "the gods themselves"); as well as adjectives expanded to form adjectival phrases, particularly participles:

The happy child squealed with delight.

Happy with his new toy, the child squealed with delight.

The defeated sailors collected their dead.

Defeated by the Athenians, the sailors collected their dead.

We must save the drowning men.

We must save the men drowning in the sea.

In all instances, however, word order is the mechanism through which the language makes clear which noun is being modified by which adjective—in most cases, the noun is modified by the adjective closest to it. Failure to observe this rule results in such grammatical irregularities as the so-called misplaced modifier:

Drowning in the sea, the captain ordered the men to be rescued.

English adjectives (with the exception of the demonstratives "this" and "that" and the intensives "himself" and "herself") lack the distinction of singular and plural forms that the nouns possess:

The young girl attracted the attention of the young boys.

Greek adjectives, like its nouns, are declined. They in fact fall into the same declensional classes as the nouns, with the same endings. The difference is that each noun typically has a unique gender and therefore has a single set of singular and plural endings. An adjective itself has no intrinsic gender but rather has different sets of forms for different genders (either all three or just two, in certain adjectives where masculine and feminine have the same endings).

These multiple forms are necessitated by the **rule of agreement**: an adjective must be in the same gender, case, and number as the noun it modifies:

ἀγαθὸς ἄνθρωπος	πᾶσαι πολεῖς
good man	all cities
ταχεῖ πλοίῳ	φευγόντων πολεμίων
with a swift ship	of fleeing enemies

You should keep three things in mind:

(1) The adjective and noun may not be in the same declension—for example, a 3rd declension adjective may modify a 2nd declension noun. In this situation (as in two of the examples above), the endings on the noun and adjective may not be the same, although they are in the same case and number.

(2) Greek does not share the English language's capacity to use nouns as adjectives, e.g., "dog food" or "wine bottle." Seemingly equivalent Greek expressions like οἰκονόμος ("housekeeper") and οἰνοχόη ("wine cup") are really single, compound nouns, as indicated by the fact that only the second element is declined.

(3) You will notice that Greek sometimes uses an adjective where in English an adverb would be expected:

ὁ Περικλῆς ἀμελῆς ἐπίστευεν τοῖς πολεμίοις
Pericles imprudently trusted his enemies.

6.1 ATTRIBUTIVE AND PREDICATIVE POSITIONS

In Greek noun phrases that contain the definite article, an adjective must be placed either between the article and noun, as is the standard case in English, or after a repetition of the article. There are thus two ways to say "the good man":

ὁ ἀγαθὸς ἀνήρ or ὁ ἀνὴρ ὁ ἀγαθός

This is called the **attributive position** of the adjective. In English, the predicative use of the adjective requires a verb, which is also an acceptable construction in Greek:

The man is good.
ὁ ἀνήρ ἐστιν ἀγαθός.

There is also the possibility, however, of omitting forms of the verb εἰμί in such sentences. This use of the adjective alone as a complete predicate is signaled by its placement *outside* of the article-noun combination, in the **predicative position**:

ὁ ἀνὴρ ἀγαθός	or	ἀγαθὸς ὁ ἀνήρ.
The man is good.		Good is the man.

6.2 DEGREES OF COMPARISON

The adjectives discussed thus far are said to be in the **positive** degree:

The teacher is wise.

The Athenians are courageous.

In the expression of a comparison, the **comparative** degree of the adjective is employed.

The teacher is wiser than the student.

The Athenians are more courageous than the Persians.

The **superlative** degree indicates the highest level of the quality in question:

Socrates is the wisest teacher.

The Spartans are the most courageous of the Greeks.

As these examples show, English forms the comparative degree by adding the suffix *-er* to short adjectives (generally either monosyllabic, or disyllabic and ending in *-y*), and using the adverb "more" with all others. Similarly, the superlative is formed by adding the suffix *-est* to shorter adjectives and using the adverb "most" with all others.

These same three degrees of adjectives are found in Greek. The positive degree is the dictionary-entry form of the adjective.

ὁ διδάσκαλος σοφός.

οἱ Ἀθηναῖοί εἰσιν ἀνδρεῖοι.

Like English, Greek forms the comparative degree by adding a suffix to the adjectival stem:

ὁ διδάσκαλος σοφώτερος ἢ ὁ μαθητής.

οἱ Ἀθηναῖοι ἀνδρειότεροί εἰσι τῶν Περσῶν.

and similarly for the superlative degree:

ὁ Σωκράτης σοφώτατος διδάσκαλός ἐστιν.

οἱ Λακεδαιμόνιοι τῶν Ἑλλήνων ἀνδρειότατοί εἰσιν.

The semantic range of the Greek comparative and superlative forms is somewhat broader than the English. In addition to meaning strictly "more," the Greek comparative can also mean "rather," or "excessively." The superlative can mean simply "very" or "exceedingly," without necessarily implying absolutely the most.

6.2.1 Irregular Comparisons: like English, Greek has a small number of adjectives whose comparative and superlative degrees are irregularly built on different stems. These are among the most common of adjectives, and you will encounter them often:

good (capable, excellent): ἀγαθός, ἀμείνων, ἄριστος

good (virtuous): ἀγαθός, βελτίων, βέλτιστος

good (strong): ἀγαθός, κρείττων, κράτιστος

good (beautiful): καλός, καλλίων, κάλλιστος

bad: κακός, κακίων, κάκιστος

bad (inferior): κακός, χείρων, χείριστος

large: μέγας, μείζων, μέγιστος

small: μικρός, ἐλάττων, ἐλάχιστος

much, many: πολύς, πλείων, πλεῖστος

few: ὀλίγος, ὀλείζων [very rare], ὀλίγιστος

swift: ταχύς, θάττων, τάχιστος

6.3 DEMONSTRATIVE ADJECTIVES

Greek demonstrative adjectives such as οὗτος ("this") and ἐκεῖνος ("that") are similar in use and meaning to their English equivalents with one exception: they are generally used in combination with the definite article. Moreover, they are usually placed in the predicative rather than the attributive position:

οὗτος ὁ ἀνήρ	or	ὁ ἀνὴρ ἐκεῖνος
this man		that man

Like any other adjective, demonstratives must agree with their nouns in gender, case, and number.

6.4 INTERROGATIVE ADJECTIVES

In English, the interrogative pronouns (see §8.5 below) are "who?" (personal) and "what?" (impersonal). Interrogative adjectives are slightly different:

Who wrote this?	vs.	What (or Which) poet wrote this?
What did you write?	vs.	What (or Which) poem did you write?

In Greek, the forms of the interrogative adjective are identical to those of the interrogative pronoun:

τίς τοῦτο ἔγραψεν;	vs.	τίς ποιητὴς τοῦτο ἔγραψεν;
τί ἔγραψας;	vs.	τί ποίημα ἔγραψας;

6.5 POSSESSIVE ADJECTIVES

Possession is most commonly indicated in English by the possessive adjectives, which are always used without an article:

My son loves your daughter.

The Athenians heard his story with pleasure.

Alternatively, but less idiomatically, the possessive adjective can be replaced by a genitival prepositional phrase:

This son of mine loves that daughter of yours.

The Athenians heard that story of his with pleasure.

For the 1st and 2nd persons, Greek has the possessive adjectives ἐμός and σός in the singular and ἡμέτερος and ὑμέτερος in the plural. In contrast to English, they are often used together with the definite article, in the attributive position:

ὁ ἐμὸς υἱὸς φιλεῖ τὴν σὴν θυγατέρα.

Much more commonly than English, however, Greek will instead employ the genitive of the personal pronoun:

ὁ υἱός μου φιλεῖ τὴν θυγατέρα σου.

This pronominal construction is always used (in Attic Greek) for the 3rd-person possessive:

οἱ Ἀθηναῖοι τὸν λόγον αὐτοῦ ἡδέως ἤκουσαν.

6.6 THE INTENSIVE ADJECTIVE αὐτός

The **intensive adjective** in English is distinctive in that, like the demonstratives and unlike other adjectives, it uses a different form for the plural:

himself, herself, itself → themselves

The English intensive must be clearly differentiated from the English reflexive pronoun:

They themselves killed. [INTENSIVE]

They killed themselves. [REFLEXIVE][1]

---

1. Note the English usage of the preposition "by" to mean "alone" or "separated from others":

They killed by themselves.

The intensive adjective in Greek, αὐτός, αὐτή, αὐτό, is only tricky because the same word can be seen in other contexts used to mean other things.[2] The word order required for the Greek intensive adjective is article/noun/adjective, all three being in agreement:

τὰς γυναῖκας αὐτάς: the women themselves

6.7 ADJECTIVES USED SUBSTANTIVELY

In English, we frequently use adjectives as nouns, often by simply adding the definite article before them. The adjectives typically refer to indefinite plural people or things, or else to an antecedent already expressed:

The land of the free [people] and the home of the brave [people]

When it comes to dinner, I prefer the quick and easy [things].

Don't give me a big wrench; I need the small [wrench].

Greek can use adjectives in essentially the same ways. Because this usage relies heavily on the definite article, it will be taken up in the next chapter.

---

2. As we'll see below (§8.1), forms of αὐτός in the oblique cases used without substantives serve as 3rd person pronouns. Also, the word-order article/αὐτός/noun is a simple adjectival phrase, meaning "the same ____":

τὰς αὐτὰς γυναῖκας: the same women

7. ARTICLES

In English, the definite article is used with a noun when the latter is being discussed as a specific entity:

We always honor the gods.

The indefinite article, which typically only occurs in the singular, marks a noun as a member of a class, without specifying which:

A god will punish the evil tyrant.

Plural nouns may be used with no article, to indicate generic groups in general statements:

Gods are more powerful than mortals.

Greek usage of the definite article (ὁ, ἡ, τό) and the indefinite (τις, τι) is analogous in the first two English examples:

ἀεὶ τιμῶμεν τοὺς θεούς.

θεός τις κολάσει τὸν κακὸν τύραννον.

However, Greek also sometimes uses the definite article to mark generic classes, as in the third example:

οἱ θεοὶ δυνατώτεροί εἰσιν τῶν θνητῶν.

Beyond this, the definite article is employed in Greek in numerous situations where it is not used in English. We have already seen its use with Greek demonstrative and possessive adjectives (§§6.3, 6.5):

ὁ ἐμὸς υἱὸς οἰκεῖ ἐν ἐκείνῃ τῇ πόλει.
My son lives in that city.

It is sometimes used with proper names of persons or places, especially in the nominative and accusative cases:

ὁ Δημοσθένης οὐ πιστεύει τῷ Φιλίππῳ.
Demosthenes does not trust Philip.

ο του Φιλίππου ἄγγελος Ἀθήναζε ἦλθεν.
Philip's messenger came to Athens.

and with abstract nouns:

<u>ἡ</u> φιλία ἰσχυρώτερα ἢ <u>τὸ</u> ἔχθος.

Love is stronger than hate.

In a sentence with a predicate nominative, English relies on word order to distinguish the subject from the predicate:

Pausanias was the general.

The general was Pausanias.

In such a sentence in Greek, both nouns will be in the nominative case. What marks the grammatical subject is not its placement before the verb but the presence of the definite article, which is not used with the predicate noun. The following sentences both mean "Pausanias was the general":

ὁ Παυσανίας στρατηγὸς ἦν.

στρατηγὸς ἦν ὁ Παυσανίας.

A distinctive feature of the Greek article is its capacity to make any word to which it is prefixed function as a noun. Most common is the making of adjectives into nouns. The English definite article shares this ability to a more limited degree. It is common with adjectives used as plural nouns in the designation of generic classes:

<u>The elderly</u> often teach <u>the young</u>

In the singular, this construction is generally restricted to rendering certain qualities as abstract nouns:

The philosopher searches for <u>the good</u> and <u>the beautiful</u>.

To indicate a single person as a member of a generic group requires a noun:

The <u>elderly person</u> often teaches the <u>young person</u>.

The Greek article has a much broader ability to make any adjective, singular or plural, into a noun:

<u>ὁ</u> γέρων πολλάκις <u>τὸν</u> νεὸν διδάσκει.

<u>οἱ</u> γέροντες πολλάκις <u>τοὺς</u> νεοὺς διδάσκουσιν.

<u>ὁ</u> φιλόσοφος ζητεῖ <u>τὸ</u> ἀγαθὸν καὶ <u>τὸ</u> καλόν.

A common use of this adjectival construction is with participles:

> ἠκούσαμεν τὰς τῶν μαχομένων βοάς.
>
> We heard the shouts of the fighters [i.e., the fighting ones].

Beyond adjectives, the article can combine with a prepositional phrase to form a noun phrase:

> οἱ ἐν τῷ οἴκῳ μάλα φοβοῦνται.
>
> Those in the house are very afraid.

or even combine with an adverb:

> οἱ ἔνδον ἐκάλεσαν τοὺς ἐκτός.
>
> Those inside called to those outside.

The infinitive of a verb (see §12) is essentially a neuter noun. With the addition of an article (the so-called articular infinitive), it can be declined and thus can play any role in the sentence that a regular noun can play:

> τὸ ἀδικεῖν μέγα κακόν ἐστιν.
>
> To act unjustly is a great evil.

> δείδω τὸ κρίνεσθαι ὑπὸ πολιτῶν ἀδίκων.
>
> I fear being judged by unjust citizens.

> πολλαὶ πόλεις λύονται τῷ μὴ τοὺς θεοὺς τιμᾶν.
>
> Many cities are destroyed by not honoring the gods.

Finally, in the very common correlative construction employing the particles μέν . . . δέ, the article alone can function as a pronoun:

> οἱ μὲν μάλα τιμῶσιν ἐκεῖνον τὸν ἄνδρα, οἱ δὲ μισοῦσιν αὐτόν.
>
> Some [people] greatly honor that man, but others hate him.

8. PRONOUNS I

The usage of pronouns, as we saw defined in Chapter 1, is fairly straightforward: pronouns are used in place of nouns. Their variety in number and their semantic complexity in both English and Greek, however, can make pronouns a challenging bit of learning. In this chapter we'll examine the most common Greek pronouns (and their English counterparts), reserving less frequent pronominal expressions for the next chapter.

All Greek pronouns exhibit the features of number and case, although not all pronouns are found in all cases. As to gender, all pronouns do exhibit gender with the exception of 1st- and 2nd-person pronouns. Not all pronouns differentiate all three genders (e.g., masculine and feminine merge in indefinite and interrogative pronouns).

Many pronouns are actually derived from related adjectives; as such, they tend to have familiar declensions (though the neuter nominative/accusative singular may end in -ο instead of -ον). True pronouns tend to have irregular declensions and must therefore be learned thoroughly.

8.1 PERSONAL PRONOUNS (SEE §2.4)

In English, the 1st-person pronouns are, in the singular, "I" (subjective), "me" (objective), and "mine" (possessive); and in the plural, "we" (subjective), "us" (objective), and "ours" (possessive):

> <u>I</u> think Socrates will welcome <u>us</u>.
>
> This shop is <u>mine</u>, but <u>we</u> can buy another.

The 2nd-person pronouns in English are "you" (subjective and objective) and "yours" (possessive). Standard modern English doesn't distinguish between singular and plural in the 2nd person, sometimes creating an ambiguity:

> <u>You</u>, Plato, think Socrates will welcome <u>you</u>.
>
> > (In this sentence, is the "you" doing the thinking, Plato, synonymous with the "you" Socrates will welcome? Perhaps Socrates will welcome Plato <u>and</u> Critias. It's impossible to know without more context or greater specificity—hence the ambiguity.)

This shop is yours, but you can buy others.

(Is this shop owned by one "you" or multiple "yous"? Will the future shops be purchased by a singular "you" or a plural "you"?)

Greek doesn't have this ambiguity because it distinguishes clearly between the 2nd singular and 2nd plural pronouns.

The 3rd-person pronoun in English distinguishes between gender in the singular: "he," "she," and "it" (subjective); "his," "hers," and "its" (possessive); and "him," "her," and "it" (objective). This distinction isn't preserved in the plural, however: "they" (subjective), "theirs" (possessive), and "them" (objective) are used for all three genders.

The books, which were theirs, they handed over to them.

In Greek, the 1st-person pronoun and the 2nd-person pronoun have rather irregular declensions in the singular. When monosyllabic and oblique, they are typically **enclitic** (that is, they don't carry their own accent); an accent is added (as well as the prefix ἐ- for the 1st-person singular pronoun), however, when the pronoun is emphatic.

μοι: to/for me [unemphatic]

λέγε δή μοι: tell me!

ἐμοί: to/for ME [emphatic]

λέγε δ' ἐμοί: tell ME!

The 3rd-person pronoun in Greek is somewhat complicated in its choices. Sometimes forms of the definite article (see §7), used without substantives, function as 3rd-person pronouns. The demonstrative adjectives ἐκεῖνος and οὗτος, used without substantives, function as 3rd-person pronouns. And finally, the intensive adjective αὐτός (see §6.6), *when used in oblique cases* without substantives, functions as a 3rd-person pronoun:

οἱ: they

οἱ ἀνεβόησαν.

They called out.

ἐκείνη: she

ἐκείνη ἡμῖν παρεῖχεν τὸ ποτόν.

She offered us water.

τοῦτο: this [subjective]

τοῦτο ἀρέσκει μοι.

This pleases me.

αὐτούς: them

πρὸς αὐτοὺς προσεβάλομεν.

We attacked them.

αὐτοῦ: his, its

ἡ θυγάτηρ αὐτοῦ καλή.

His daughter is beautiful.

ἡ ἀρχὴ αὐτοῦ ἦν παλαιοτάτη.

Its origin was very ancient.

αὐταῖς: to them (feminine)

παρέχω αὐταῖς παραμυθίαν.

I offer consolation to them.

Like English, Greek does not distinguish gender with 1st- and 2nd-person pronouns—that distinction only occurs with the 3rd-person pronoun (in English, only in the singular of the 3rd-person pronoun).

In Greek, more than English, the so-called "plural of majesty" (a.k.a. "royal plural" or "nosism") occurs with the 1st-person pronoun. This usage is most common in self-reference by an author:

τιμῶσιν ἡμᾶς.

They honor us [that is, me].

ἡμεῖς τιμῶμέν σε.

We [that is, I] honor you.

Compared with English, Greek only infrequently uses the 2nd-person pronoun impersonally for imaginary persons:

γνῶθι σεαυτόν.

Know thyself!

Greek would more commonly express this idea with a 3rd-person construction:

πᾶς τις γνώτω ἑαυτόν.

Let each person know himself!

8.2 REFLEXIVE PRONOUNS

As they refer back to the subject of the clause or sentence, **reflexive pronouns** occur only in the oblique cases in the predicate, and they combine forms of the personal pronouns with forms of the intensive adjective (see §6.6).

1st-person reflexive: in the singular, there is a **crasis** (the contraction of a vowel ending one word with the vowel beginning the next word) of ἐμ- (the 1st-person pronoun) with αὐτοῦ, αὐτῆς, etc.:

ἐμαυτῷ: to/for myself

ποιῶ ἐμαυτῷ τοῦτο.

I do this for myself.

In the plural, both the personal pronoun and the intensive are written as separate words: ἡμῶν αὐτῶν "of ourselves," etc.

2nd-person reflexive: in the singular, either a compound consisting of the 2nd-person pronominal σε- prefixing αὐτοῦ, αὐτῆς, etc., or a crasis of the two elements:

σεαυτόν or σαυτόν: yourself

σῷζε σαυτόν.

Save yourself!

In the plural, both the personal pronoun and the intensive are written as separate words: ὑμῶν αὐτῶν "of yourselves," etc.

3rd-person reflexive: in both the singular and plural, either a compound consisting of the archaic 3rd-person pronominal ἑ- prefixing αὐτοῦ, αὐτῆς, etc., or a crasis of the two elements:

ἑαυτοῦ or αὑτοῦ: of himself

λέξει ὑπὲρ ἑαυτοῦ.

He will speak on behalf of himself.

ἑαυτούς or αὑτούς: themselves

νικῶσιν αὑτούς.

They are defeating themselves.

8.3 DEMONSTRATIVE PRONOUNS

The most common demonstratives in Greek are offered by forms of ἐκεῖνος ("that") and οὗτος ("this").

> αἱρούμεθα ταῦτα ἀντὶ ἐκείνων.
>
> We prefer these [things] to those [things].

Nearly as common is the pronoun ὅδε, ἥδε, τόδε (the definite article + the demonstrative suffix -δε), meaning "the [one/s] here."

> ἐπράττομεν τάδε ὑπὲρ τῶνδε.
>
> We were doing these [things] on behalf of these [people].

8.4 RELATIVE PRONOUNS (SEE §2.4)

Keep in mind that besides serving as pronouns, **relative pronouns** also have the syntactical function of a subordinating conjunction (see §§19 and 28.2):

> We can't trust that man who talks of peace but prepares for war.

The relative pronoun here introduces the subordinate clause ("talks of peace but prepares for war").

In English, the relative pronouns "who," "whom," "which," "whose," and "that" do not distinguish between singular and plural. "Who," "whom," and "whose" are masculine or feminine; "which" is typically neuter; "that" can be used for any gender; and "whose" can be used for neuters where "of which" sounds awkward. Finally, in terms of proper case, "who," "which," and "that" are subjective case; "whose," and "of which" are possessive; and "whom," "which," and "that" are objective.

Greek employs an array of different relatives. When translating the Greek relative into English, you must take great care with the proper choice of "who," "whom," "which," "whose," and "of which."

The **simple relative** pronoun is ὅς, ἥ, ὅ which is declined like the definite article except with the omission of the initial τ-:

> ὁ ἀνὴρ ὃς ἐθαύμαζε τὸν Περικλέα ἀπέθανεν.
>
> The man who admired Pericles died.

ὁ ἀνὴρ ὃν ὁ Περικλῆς ἐθαύμαζεν ἀπέθανεν.
The man whom Pericles admired died.

For the syntactical rules governing the use of relative pronouns within independent and dependent clauses, see §19.

8.5 INTERROGATIVE PRONOUNS

The interrogative pronoun in English closely resembles the relative pronoun in form, except that "that" isn't used, while "what" (neuter, subjective, or objective) is. In terms of usage, interrogative pronouns are used to ask direct questions and indirect questions:

Who are you?

Whom do they seek?

Whose poem were you listening to?

I ask who you are.

I ask whom they seek.

I ask whose poem you were listening to.

The **simple interrogative** pronoun in Greek can be distinguished from the simple indefinite (see next) by its accent: it is always acute, and it is always on the penult (second-to-last syllable) for disyllabic forms: τίς, τί, τίνας, τίνων, τίσι, etc.

τίς εἶ;
Who are you?

τίνας ζητοῦσιν;
Whom do they seek?

τὸ ποίημα τίνος ἠκούεσθε;
Whose poem were you listening to?

8.6 INDEFINITE PRONOUNS

In English, the **indefinite pronouns** are "some," "any," "a certain [one]," "someone," "somebody," "something," "anyone," "anybody," and "anything."

"Any" and its compounds are true indefinites in that they refer to persons or things unknown. "Some" and its compounds and "a certain [one]" can refer to persons or things whose actual identities are known but not specified or disclosed.

English also has the **emphatic indefinites**: "no matter who/whom/whose/what/which"; "whoever," "whomever," "whosever," "whatever," "whichever," "whosoever," "whomsoever," and "whatsoever."

As for Greek, great care must be exercised in distinguishing the **simple indefinite** pronoun from the interrogative pronoun, which it very closely resembles. Accent presents the best means for distinction. The simple indefinite is enclitic; if the word must carry an accent due to its context, that accent will always be a grave or circumflex for monosyllabic forms or an acute or circumflex on the ultima (last syllable) for disyllabic forms: τις, τι or, if an accent is required, τὶς, τὶ (contrast interrogatives: τίς, τί); τινα, τινες, τινων or, if an accent is required, τινά, τινές, τινῶν (contrast interrogatives: τίνα, τίνες, τίνων).

τινές εἰσιν ἄπληστοι.	Some [people] are greedy.
τινά ἔδομεν τοῖς τέκνοις.	We gave some[things] to the children.
ἀσπάσεται τὶς τὸν στρατηγόν.	Someone will greet the general.[1]

Negative indefinite pronouns: οὐδείς (or μηδείς), οὐδεμία (or μηδεμία), οὐδέν (or μηδέν), etc., and the more poetic, οὔτις, οὔτι, οὔτινος, etc., "no one," "nobody," "none," "nothing":[2]

ποθεῖς ἀποκρίσεις, ἀλλὰ δὲ οὐδεμία ἀρέσει σοι.
You want answers, but none will please you.

1. Now contrast:

τίνες εἰσιν ἄπληστοι;	Who [which people] are greedy?
τίνα ἔδομεν τοῖς τέκνοις;	What [things] did we give to the children?
ἀσπάσεται τίς τὸν στρατηγόν;	Who will greet the general?

2. For when forms of μηδείς and μήτις should be used in place of forms of οὐδείς and οὔτις, see §11.6.

οὔτι ἀρέσει σοι.
Nothing will please you.

Greek, too, has **emphatic indefinites**, which are forms of the indefinite relative pronoun (see §9.2.3) plus the suffix -οῦν:

ἀσπάσεται ὁστισοῦν τὸν στρατηγόν.
Anyone whosoever will greet the general.

ἅτιναοῦν ἔδομεν τοῖς τέκνοις.
We gave whatsoever to the children.

8.7 POSSESSIVE PRONOUNS

In Greek, the genitives of the personal, demonstrative, and reflexive pronouns often serve as the possessive pronouns. Alternatively, a possessive adjective (based on the personal pronouns) can be used (see §6.5).

your speeches, the speeches of yours: οἱ λόγοι ὑμέτεροι or οἱ λόγοι ὑμῶν

The following chart will help systematize some of the information from this chapter:

PERSONAL PRONOUNS

	1st Person	2nd Person	3rd Person
SIMPLE	ἐγώ(ν)/ἡμεῖς, etc.	σύ/ὑμεῖς, etc.	article/demonstrative/ intensive
EMPHATIC	μοῦ, μοί, μέ ἐμοῦ, ἐμοί, ἐμέ	σοῦ, σοί, σέ	αὐτός, αὐτή, αὐτό, etc.
REFLEXIVE	ἐμαυτοῦ, etc. ἡμῶν αὐτῶν, etc.	σεαυτοῦ or σαυτοῦ, etc. ὑμῶν αὐτῶν, etc.	ἑαυτοῦ or αὑτοῦ, etc. ἑαυτῶν or αὑτῶν, etc.
POSSESSIVE	μου/ἡμῶν	σου/ὑμῶν	αὐτοῦ, αὐτῆς, αὐτοῦ, αὐτῶν τούτου, ταύτης, τούτου, τούτων ἐκείνου, ἐκείνης, ἐκείνου, ἐκείνων

9. PRONOUNS II

In the previous chapter, we surveyed the most common Greek pronouns, establishing most of the pronoun types and many of their varieties. In the present chapter, we examine the remaining types and varieties.

9.1 DEMONSTRATIVE PRONOUNS (SEE §8.3)

Forms of the definite article, when used alone without a substantive, can function as a weak demonstrative:

οἱ μὲν ἀνεβόησαν, οἱ δὲ ἐκάθευδον.
These called out, but those were sleeping.

9.1.1 Deictic: The **deictic**[1] suffix -ι can be added to any demonstrative pronoun for emphasis:

οὑτοσί: this one here
οὑτοσὶ τάχα ἀποχωρήσει.
This one here will soon depart.

ἐκειναιί: those [women] there
ἐκειναιὶ ἐτίμων τὴν θεόν.
Those women there honored the goddess.

When the demonstrative ends in -α, -ε, or -ο, these vowels are omitted before the addition of the deictic suffix:

τοῦτο → τουτί: this [thing] here
τουτὶ οὐκ ἐποιήσαμεν.
This [thing] here we didn't do.

τοῦδε → τουδί: of this [one] here
τὰ πράγματα τουδί ἐστιν αἰσχρά.
The affairs of this one here are disgraceful.

1. **Deictic**, from the Greek δείκνυναι (to show), means *directly* pointing out or indicating, as if one's pointing a linguistic finger at a person or object.

9.1.2 Quantitative: Greek also has the **quantitative demonstratives** τοσόσδε and τοσοῦτος, derived from adjectives, meaning "so big," "so much," "such."

οὐδεὶς δύναται τοσάδε πάσχειν.

No one can endure such great [things].

τοσούτους οὐδέποτε ἑωράκεμεν.

We had never seen so many [people].

9.1.3 Qualitative: Finally, there is a **qualitative demonstrative** τοιοῦτος, also derived from an adjective, meaning "such," "of such a type," "of such a sort."

οὐδεὶς δύναται τοιοῦτα πάσχειν.

No one can endure things of such a type.

τοιούτους οὐδέποτε ἑωράκεμεν.

We had never seen such [people].

9.2 RELATIVE PRONOUNS (SEE §8.4)

9.2.1 Intensive: Greek has an **intensive relative** pronoun with the addition of the enclitic suffix -περ to the simple relative:

ὅσπερ: the very one who

ὁ Εὐριπίδης ἐστίν ὅσπερ ἀπεχώρησεν.

Euripides is the very one who departed.

ὧνπερ: the very ones whose

οἱ Ἀθηναῖοι ἐπέβαλον πρὸς τοὺς Μηλίους ὧνπερ ἡ νῆσος ἦν μικρά.

The Athenians attacked the Melians, the very ones whose island was small.

9.2.2 Contingent: Also found in Greek is a **contingent relative** with the addition of the enclitic suffix -τε to the simple relative:

ὅτε: inasmuch as it, provided that it, so long as it

ὁ Δημοσθένης ἐπαινεῖ τὸ χρῆμα ὅτε ἀρέσκει τῇ ἐκκλησίᾳ.

Demosthenes approves the matter provided it pleases the assembly.

9.2.3 Indefinite/General: Consider now the **indefinite relative** (also called the **general relative**), which is a compound of the simple relative (§8.4) plus the simple indefinite pronoun (§8.6), where *both* elements are declined: ὅστις, ἥτις, ὅ τι; οὗτινος, ἧστινος, οὗτινος (or ὅτου); etc.: "anyone who," "anything which," "whoever," "whichever," "whosoever," "whatsoever."

ἡ ἐκκλησία παρέχει τιμὴν ᾧτινι βουλή.

The assembly pays honor to anyone the council does.

οἱ Μῆδοι ἐφείδοντο ἐκείνων οἵτινες συνεχώρησαν.

The Persians spared those whosoever surrendered.

9.2.4 Quantitative: Greek employs a **quantitative relative** pronoun ὅσος, "as much as," "as many as," or "as big as."

ὁ Ἀλέξανδρος οὐ σπουδάσει περὶ τούτους τοὺς ἵππους ὅσοι γίγνονται.

Alexander won't interest himself in these horses, as big as they become.

9.2.5 Qualitative: And finally, there is a Greek **qualitative relative** pronoun, οἷος, οἷα, οἷον, "such as," "of which kind."

ὁ Ἀλέξανδρος οὐ σπουδάσει περὶ ἵππους οἷοι οὗτοι γίγνονται.

Alexander won't interest himself in horses such as these become.

9.3 INTERROGATIVE PRONOUNS (SEE §8.5)

9.3.1 Quantitative: The **quantitative interrogative**, based on an adjective, is πόσος, "how big?," "how much?."

ἐναντίος πόσοις ἠγόρευεν;

In front of how many did he speak?

πόσον ἦν νικᾶν τοὺς Πέρσας;

How big [a thing] was it to defeat the Persians?

9.3.2 Qualitative: The **qualitative interrogative**, also based on an adjective, is ποῖος, "what sort of?," "of what kind?."

ποῖα δυνάμεθα πάσχειν;

What [kind of things] can we endure?

ποίους εἴδετε;

What sort [of people] did you see?

9.4 INDEFINITE PRONOUNS (SEE §8.6)

9.4.1 Generalizing Indefinite: English's most common **generalizing indefinite** pronouns are "everyone," "everybody," "everything," "each," and "all."

Greek's **generalizing indefinite** pronoun, πάς, πᾶσα, πάν, "all," "entire," "every," is based on the generalizing indefinite adjective πάς, πᾶσα, πάν.[2]

πάντες χαλεπῶς φέρουσι τὸν Σωκράτην.

All [people] are annoyed by Socrates.

Besides πάς, πᾶσα, πάν, Greek's most common generalizing pronouns are ἕκαστος, ἑκάστη, ἕκαστον ("each"), and ἑκάτερος, ἑκατέρη, ἑκάτερον ("each of two"):

ἑκατέρῳ ἔδομεν: we gave to each of two

ἕκαστος ἦν ἐλεύθερος: each/everyone/everybody was free

9.5 COMPARATIVE PRONOUNS

Comparative pronouns are exclusively used when two persons or objects are referred to. The Greek ones found here, all derived from adjectives, have no simple counterparts in English.

2. Made definite with the addition of a genitive: πάντες τῶν Ἀθηναίων χαλεπῶς φέρουσι τὸν Σωκράτην: "All of the Athenians are annoyed by Socrates."

9.5.1 Comparative Demonstrative: The **comparative demonstrative** pronouns are ἕτερος used with the definite article ("the other of two") and οὐδέτερος/μηδέτερος,[3] ("neither of two").

αἱρήσασθε τὸ ἕτερον.
Choose the other one!

αἱρήσασθε μηδέτερον.
Choose neither!

9.5.2 Comparative Interrogative: The **comparative interrogative** pronoun is πότερος, "which of two?"

ποτέρᾳ ἐχρᾶτο;
Which [i.e. of his hands] did he use?

9.5.3 Comparative Relative: The **comparative relative** pronoun ὁπότερος, "whichever of the two," is used in Greek.

αἱρήσασθε ὁπότερον ἀρέσκει ὑμῖν.
Choose whichever pleases you.

9.5.4 Comparative Indefinite: Lastly, we come to the Greek **comparative indefinite** pronoun: ποτερός ("whichever of the two," "some(one) of two").

ἐχρᾶτο ποτερᾷ.
He used whichever [i.e. hand].

9.6 PARTICULARIZING PRONOUNS

Particularizing pronouns in English run a wide gamut: "each," "either," "neither," "both," "the other," "the only," "none." Unlike Greek, English doesn't always distinguish with its pronouns between duals and plurals: "each of two" or "each of several"; "the other of two" or "the other of several"; "the only of two" or "the only of several." But sometimes it does: "either [of two]," "neither [of two]," "both [of two]," "none [of several]."

3. See §11.6 for the contexts where μηδέτερος replaces οὐδέτερος.

Greek offers a number of common particularizing pronouns, all derived from adjectives; e.g.,

ἕτερος used with the definite article: "the other of two" (see §9.5.1)

ἑκάτερος: "either of two"

μόνος: "the only," "the sole," "the one alone"

οὐδέτερος/μηδέτερος: "neither of two" (see §9.5.1)

9.6.1 Indefinite Particularizing: Greek's **indefinite particularizing** pronoun, ἄλλος, ἄλλη, ἄλλο ("another," "an [indefinite] other," "some other") is based on the indefinite particularizing adjective ἄλλος, ἄλλη, ἄλλο. Also, ἕτερος used without the definite article is used to mean "another of two."

τοῦτο ἄχρηστον· δὸς δή μοι ἄλλο.
This is worthless; give me another.

9.7 RECIPROCAL PRONOUN

The Greek reciprocal pronoun is only used in the plural (or dual) in the oblique cases: ἀλλήλων, ἀλλήλοις, etc.[4] ("of each other," "to/for each other," etc.)

εἶδον ἀλλήλους
they saw each other

9.8 INDIRECT PRONOUNS

Greek has a distinct group of pronouns not found in English: **indirect pronouns**. These are used in the specific context of indirect questions. They are typically formed by adding the prefix ὁ- or ὁσ-, commonly seen with indefinite

4. Created from a doubling of the particularizing indefinite adjective ἄλλος (see above): thus "other/other."

relative pronouns (see above, §9.2.3), to the various interrogative pronouns (see §§8.5, 9.3); e.g.,

τίς → ὅστις

τίς βαίνει; → γιγνώσκω ὅστις βαίνει

who is coming? → I know who is coming

πότερος → ὁπότερος

πότερος βαίνει;→ γιγνώσκω ὁπότερος βαίνει

which [of the two] is coming? → I know which [of the two] is coming

πόσος → ὁπόσος

πόσοι βαίνουσιν; → γιγνώσκω ὁπόσοι βαίνουσιν

how many are coming? → I know how many are coming

ποῖος → ὁποῖος

ποῖοι βαίνουσιν; → γιγνώσκω ὁποῖοι βαίνουσιν

What sorts are coming? → I know what sorts are coming

To be sure, the extensive battery of Greek pronouns can seem a bit overwhelming. It may be useful to visualize this pronominal system as a spectrum: the categories differentiated above simply name the primary colors, and each individual pronoun represents a particular hue which blends and blurs into the pronouns which are semantically closest to it. This subtle coloration exhibited by the pronominal system provides us with a great insight into one of the niceties of the Greek language.

The following chart will help systematize most of the information from this chapter and some of the information from the previous chapter:

PRONOUNS

	DEMONSTRATIVE	RELATIVE	INDEFINITE	INTERROGATIVE	INDIRECT
SIMPLE	οὗτος, αὕτη, τοῦτο ἐκεῖνος, ἐκείνη, ἐκεῖνο ὅδε, ἥδε, τόδε	ὅς, ἥ, ὅ	τις, τι	τίς, τί	ὅστις, ἥτις, ὅ τι
negative			οὔτις, οὔτι* οὐδείς, οὐδεμία, οὐδέν*		
EMPHATIC-INTENSIVE	οὑτοσί, etc. ἐκεινοσί, etc. ὁδί, ἡδί, τοδί	ὅσπερ, ἥπερ, ὅπερ	ὁστισοῦν, ἡτισοῦν, ὁτιοῦν		
QUANTITATIVE	τοσόσδε, etc. τοσοῦτος, etc.	ὅσος, ὅση, ὅσον	ποσός, ποσή, ποσόν	πόσος, πόση, πόσον	ὁπόσος, etc.
QUALITATIVE	τοιοῦτος, etc.	οἷος, οἷα, οἷον	ποιός, ποιά, ποιόν	ποῖος, ποῖα, ποῖον	ὁποῖος, etc.
COMPARATIVE	ἕτερος, etc.	ὁπότερος, etc.	ποτερός, etc.	πότερος, etc.	ὁπότερος, etc.
negative	οὐδέτερος, etc.*				
GENERALIZING	ἑκάτερος, etc.	ὅστις, ἥτις, ὅ τι	ὅστις, ἥτις, ὅ τι πᾶς, πᾶσα, πᾶν ἕκαστος, etc.		
PARTICULARIZING	μόνος, etc. ἑκάτερος, etc.		ἕτερος, etc. ἄλλος, ἄλλη, ἄλλο		
CONTINGENT		ὅστε, ἥτε, ὅτε			

* NOTE: For those contexts where forms of μήτις, μηδείς, and μηδέτερος are used, see §11.6.

10. PREPOSITIONS

A preposition is a word used in a phrase with a noun (or its equivalent) expressing that noun's relationship to another word or idea. Among the more common such relationships in English are the following:

Location:	The farmer is in the field.
Direction:	The ship is sailing into the harbor. The thieves are running from the house.
Possession:	The words of a philosopher are wise.
Time:	We sailed for three days. We arrived on the fourth day.
Agent:	This drama was written by Sophocles.
Means:	They killed the wolf with stones.
Manner:	We heard the report with great fear.
Accompaniment:	I will go to the agora with my brother.

The substantive in the prepositional phrase is called the **object of the preposition**. In English, if the object is a pronoun, it will be in the objective rather than the subjective case:

The dog is running toward him.

This is just between you and me.

Will you come with us?

In many situations, Greek use of the preposition is quite similar. The object of a preposition is always one of the three oblique cases. Some prepositions can be used with two or even all three cases, with different meanings with each case. The correct usage will be indicated as part of the dictionary entry for the preposition.

The following Greek prepositional constructions are analogous to the English examples listed above:

Location:	ὁ γεωργὸς ἐν τῷ ἀγρῷ ἐστιν.
Direction:	τὸ πλοῖον πλεῖ εἰς τὸν λιμένα. οἱ κλέπται ἀπὸ τοῦ οἴκου τρέχουσιν.

Agent: τοῦτο τὸ δρᾶμα ὑπὸ τοῦ Σοφοκλέους ἐγράφη.

Accompaniment: εἶμι πρὸς τὴν ἀγορὰν μετὰ τοῦ ἀδελφοῦ.

In many other situations, however, we have seen (§5) that it is the declensional ending of the noun that indicates its relationship to other parts of the sentence, thereby rendering the use of a preposition unnecessary. This is true for the remaining examples in the list above:

Possession: οἱ φιλοσόφου λόγοι φρόνιμοι.

Time: ἐπλεύσαμεν τρεῖς ἡμέρας.
ἀφικόμεθα τῇ τρίτῃ ἡμέρᾳ.

Means: τὸν λύκον ἀπέκτειναν τοῖς λίθοις.

Manner: τὴν ἀγγελίαν ἠκούσαμεν μεγάλῳ φόβῳ.

When translating such sentences from Greek into English, you will need to include the appropriate English preposition, even though there is none in the Greek.

Two things to keep in mind:

(1) The semantic ranges of seemingly equivalent prepositions in the two languages are at best overlapping but never identical. Consider the case of the English "with" in the examples above. When it expresses means or manner, it is translated in Greek by a noun in the dative case, with no preposition; when it expresses accompaniment, it is translated by the Greek preposition μετά with the genitive case (or sometimes σύν with the dative).

Particularly hazardous is the English word "to." It can be used to mark a noun or pronoun as an indirect object, whereas Greek simply puts the noun in the dative case:

We give gifts to the gods.
δῶρα τοῖς θεοῖς δίδομεν.

It can be used prepositionally to indicate the goal of motion:

The army was marching to the sea.
τὸ στράτευμα ἐπορεύετο πρὸς τὴν θάλατταν.

It is also used to form an infinitive, a grammatical form that Greek creates through inflection:

I want to marry a goddess.
βούλομαι γαμεῖν θεάν.

(2) Many verbs in English govern prepositional phrases, where the Greek equivalent takes a simple accusative direct object:

The strangers were looking at the temple.
οἱ ξένοι ἔβλεπον τὸ ἱερόν.

The people were listening to the speech of the orator.
ὁ δῆμος ἤκουε τοὺς τοῦ ῥήτορος λόγους.

When translating from English to Greek, be sure not to use a prepositional phrase with such verbs.

Occasionally words functioning as prepositions will be placed after the noun they govern. They are then said to be **postpositive**. The true preposition περί is so used in Attic prose (when it is accented πέρι), and others more commonly so in poetry (in a figure called **anastrophe**). When the words ἕνεκα ("on account of") and χάριν ("for the sake of") function as prepositions, they are regularly postpositive.

In a poetic figure called **tmesis**, the prepositional prefix of a compound verb can occasionally be written separately from its stem. Care should be exercised here in recognizing that the nouns of the clause are *not* serving as the object of this seeming preposition.

ἐν δ᾽ ἐδύσατο χαλκόν (= ἐνεδύσατο δὲ χαλκόν): he donned his bronze

ἡμῖν ἀπὸ λοιγὸν ἀμῦναι (= ἡμῖν λοιγὸν ἀπαμῦναι): to fend off destruction from us

III. THE SYNTAX OF VERBS AND RELATED ELEMENTS

11. VERBS

A verb is the word which expresses the acting, being, doing, etc., in a clause or sentence. Like nouns, a verb as a vocabulary item carries a semantic meaning, but it takes on a variety of different forms which indicate its precise syntactic role in the sentence or clause. Whereas a listing of all the forms of a noun is called its declension, for a verb this listing is called its **conjugation**, and to make such a list is to **conjugate** the verb. As was also true in the case of nouns, unfortunately not all verbs use the same set of endings. All verbs belong to one of two conjugations, called **thematic** (that is, relying on consistent vowel[s]) and **athematic** (relying on no consistent vowel).

Remember, verbs can be action verbs, linking verbs, or auxiliary verbs; see §2.6.

We saw that two things are needed to specify a particular noun form: case and number; for an adjective, with the addition of gender, three things are required. For verbs, the number is five:

Person (3): 1st, 2nd, or 3rd

Number (3): singular, dual (rare in Attic Greek), or plural

Tense (7): present, future, imperfect, aorist, perfect, pluperfect, or future perfect.

Voice (3): active, middle, or passive

Mood (4): indicative, imperative, optative, or subjunctive

So, for example, the phrase "3rd-person plural aorist active optative" will designate a unique verb form.

English verbs have one of the simplest inflectional systems of any European language. For regular verbs, the only suffixes are *-(e)s* in the present and *-(e)d* in the past. All other designations of tense, mood, or voice are formed with the auxiliary verbs: am, is, are, was, were, be, been, have, has, had, do, does, did, will, would, shall, and should. By contrast, apart from a few forms in the perfect system, Greek only rarely uses auxiliary verbs but rather makes indications of person, number, tense, voice, and mood through the use of affixes, infixes, and/or stem alterations.

In English, a relatively small number of irregular verbs make changes in the stem to form past tenses, such as know, knew, known; or sink, sank, sunk. In order to use these verbs correctly in sentences, it is necessary to know all three of these forms, which are called the **principal parts** of the verb. Because they are unpredictable (if sink, sank, sunk, then why link, linked, linked and not link, lank, lunk?), they are provided by the dictionary entry for the verb and must be learned as part of English vocabulary.

What is the exception in English is the rule in Greek. Although there are some groups of verbs that are regular, in the sense that knowing one form will enable you to produce all others, this is generally not the case. Greek normally requires six pieces of information in order to produce all forms of a given verb: the stems to be used for the present, future, aorist, aorist passive, perfect, and perfect passive tenses. These six principal parts are provided by a Greek vocabulary or dictionary (though not all verbs have all six). The order in which these forms are listed may vary slightly in different textbooks or dictionaries, but the first form will always be the same: the verb will always be listed under the 1st-person singular, present active indicative form. For example:

πέμπω, πέμψω, ἔπεμψα, ἐπέμφθην, πέπομφα, πέπεμμαι.

11.1 TRANSITIVE AND INTRANSITIVE USAGE

Verbs are classified as **transitive** or **intransitive** (a characteristic generally indicated for verbal entries in English dictionaries by the abbreviations *tr.* or *intr.*). A **transitive** verb is one that can govern a direct object, which serves to complete its meaning:

Everyone praised the poet.

πάντες ἐπῄνησαν τὸν ποιητήν.

An **intransitive** verb cannot govern a direct object. The most common intransitive verb is the verb *to be* (εἰμί); most verbs of motion are also intransitive:

Homer was a poet.
ὁ Ὅμηρος ἦν ποιητής.

Everyone went up to the Acropolis.
πάντες ἀνέβησαν εἰς τὴν ἀκρόπολιν.

In each of these two examples of intransitive verbs, the verb is also joined by other words which complete its meaning, but in neither instance do we see a direct object: in the first example we have a predicate noun, and in the second a prepositional phrase. In Greek, this means that an intransitive verb will not govern as direct object a substantive in *the accusative case.*

In English many verbs can be used both transitively and intransitively with no distinction in form:

He turned his chair to face the speaker.

He turned when he heard a noise behind him.

I walk the dog every morning.

I walk to school when the weather is nice.

There is no inflectional marker on the verb itself to indicate whether it is being used transitively or intransitively. Greek also has such verbs, but as we shall see in the discussion of voice (§11.5), different forms of these verbs are used to make this distinction.

11.1.1 FINE POINTS

We defined transitive verbs as verbs which can take a direct object; intransitive verbs cannot take a direct object. Similarly, sentences can be described as transitive (having a direct object in the main predicate) or intransitive (not having a direct object in the main predicate). This distinction between transitive and intransitive is a useful taxonomic convenience, but it's very inexact and has little real or intrinsic semantic or psychological significance.

Even though a verb *can* take a direct object, it doesn't always do so. When a verb is the only constituent part of a sentence's predicate, it's said to be used **absolutely**. When a verb is used in an expanded predicate which doesn't include a direct object, it's said to be used **intransitively**. And when a verb is used in a predicate that does include a direct object, it's said to be used **transitively**. These claims are also true for Greek verbs.

They sang. [ABSOLUTE USE]

They sang out of tune. [INTRANSITIVE USE]

They sang a Welsh folk tune. [TRANSITIVE USE]

Care must be exercised with Greek verbs, however, because often when a verb is used absolutely or intransitively, the English verb used to translate it can be different from the English used to translate the same verb when transitive. E.g.,

νικῶσιν.	They are winning.
ῥαδίως νικῶσιν.	They are winning easily.
νικῶσιν τοὺς Λακεδαιμονίους.	They are defeating the Spartans.

Sometimes a verb which is normally intransitive can be observed to be transitive in a particular restricted usage. This claim is also true for some Greek verbs. E.g.,

I walked in the road.

I walked the dog in the road.

The verb "walk" is usually intransitive, except when it means "to take someone or something for a walk," in which case it is transitive.

Some Greek verbs, commonly used intransitively, can also often be found used transitively; if the equivalent verb in English is intransitive, the addition of a preposition into your translation will be required. E.g., the verb χαίρω (I rejoice) is normally intransitive, but when it's occasionally used transitively, it must be translated "I rejoice at."

An intransitive verb compounded with a prepositional prefix may become transitive. The verb ἔρχομαι, for example, is always intransitive; but when it's compounded with ἐπί and becomes ἐπέρχομαι, it can become transitive. The compounded verb, however, may also be used with a repeated preposition, rendering the verb intransitive again. Consider,

ἐπερχόμεθα τοὺς πολεμίους: we are attacking the enemy [TRANSITIVE]

ἐπερχόμεθα ἐπὶ τοὺς πολεμίους: we are attacking the enemy [INTRANSITIVE]

Some Greek verbs can be observed to be used either transitively or intransitively, with no discernible difference in meaning. The verb μέμφομαι, to cite just one example, can be found with a personal object in either the accusative or dative, and in either case it means "to blame someone."

11.2 DEVERBATIVES

Both English and Greek contain a number of **deverbatives**. These words are derived from verbs but function syntactically as nouns or adjectives. For example, in English we find:

Active participle: <u>Hearing</u> a noise, I went out to investigate.

Passive participle: <u>Summoned</u> by the teacher, the students returned to the classroom.

Gerund[1]: By <u>rowing</u> swiftly, the Athenian fleet reached Mitylene just in time.

Infinitive: Not all citizens wanted <u>to honor</u> Pericles.

As these examples show, although they are functioning as nouns or adjectives, the verbal nature of deverbatives allows them to employ some of the syntax of verbs as well: governing direct objects, for example, or taking adverbial modification.

1. A **gerund** is a deverbative noun, which in English always bears the suffix *-ing*.

Greek frequently employs infinitives (§12) and participles (§13), but has no gerund. It does have two further verbal derivatives: adjectives ending in -τός can function as a perfect passive participle, or indicate possibility (like English *-able*); those ending in -τέος denote necessity (§15).

11.3 PERSON AND NUMBER

On the model of classical languages, English verbs have traditionally been said to have three persons. The concept of **person** isn't often reflected in the main verb itself but rather in the pronouns or nouns serving as the subject of the verb:

I walk

we sing

we were listening

I will speak

In the preceding examples, the persons are 1st person, as exhibited by the use of the 1st-person pronouns in the subjective case.

you walk

you [plural] sing

you [plural] were listening

you will speak

These are all 2nd persons, as exhibited by the use of the 2nd-person pronoun in the subjective case. Notice how there is no difference between the 1st and 2nd persons *in the verbs themselves*; *the difference lies in the personal pronouns* (see §8.1).

Examples of the 3rd person are:

she walks

they sing

the people were listening

the politician will speak

In these, the use of both nouns and 3rd-person pronouns in the subjective case reveals that the verbs are 3rd person.

Notice that in the 3rd person (singular only) the inflection on the main verb or one of its auxiliaries can change:

I walk → she walks

you were walking → he was walking

they are walking → it is walking

we have walked → she has walked

you [plural] do walk → he does walk

But:

I walked → she walked

The feature of number is also present for English verbs. But, again, it is exhibited more by the nouns and pronouns of verbs' subjects than by the inflections on the verbs themselves. In fact, there is no verb inflection in English that specifically signifies number, except for the *-(e)s* suffix generally used in the present singular of the 3rd person (see the examples just above).

As is the case with English nouns, verbs in English reflect the numbers of singular and plural, but only in the 3rd-person present. (In other tenses, the distinction may be made by means of the auxiliaries: I was coming → we were coming.)

To put a fine point on the matter, the only English verb inflection pertaining to person and number is *-(e)s*, which is placed on the 3rd-person singular of simple present verbs; thus, one might say, the English verb actually has only two persons: 3rd singular (in the present only) and all others.[2]

(I) walk	(we) walk
(you) walk	(you all) walk
(he/she/it) walks	(they) walk

2. The only exceptions to this are the verb "to be," which uses "am" in the 1st-person present and "was" in the 1st and 3rd persons past; the auxiliary verb "will," according to formal English grammar, is used in the 2nd and 3rd persons (singular and plural), but is to be replaced by "shall" in the 1st person (singular and plural).

Greek verbs have the same three persons traditionally (though anachronistically) ascribed to English verbs (that is, 1st, 2nd, and 3rd) and distinguish between all of them by means of inflectional endings. Moreover, in addition to singular and plural, Greek verbs can also specify the dual number. The dual, however, can only be expressed in the 2nd person and in the 3rd person (there are no 1st-person dual endings; the 1st-person plural endings are used instead); and, as we saw in the case of the dual number for nouns, the dual in verbs is rare in Attic Greek and drops completely out of use after ca. 300 BCE.[3]

βαδίζω: I walk

ὑμνοῦμεν: we sing

ἤκουες: you were listening

ἀγορεύσετε: you [plural] will speak

βεβάδικε: he/she/it has walked

ὕμνησαν: they did sing

Several things should be borne in mind with person and number for Greek verbs. First, subjects consisting of collective nouns, which though semantically plural are grammatically singular, are usually construed with singular verbs. Second, in a seeming anomaly, neuter plural subjects in Greek commonly take 3rd-person *singular* verbs:

The people are angry. τὸ πλῆθός ἐστι πικρόν.

These books are beautiful. ταῦτα τὰ βιβλία ἐστί καλά.

Third, compound subjects in Greek, as in English, typically take plural verbs. A 1st-person plural verb is used if one of the subjects is 1st person; a 2nd-person plural verb is used if one or more of the subjects is 2nd person:

Xenophon and Plato were Socrates' students.
ὁ Ξενοφῶν καὶ ὁ Πλάτων ἦσαν μαθηταὶ τοῦ Σωκράτους.

Plato and I were Socrates' students.
ἐγὼ καὶ ὁ Πλάτων ἦμεν μαθηταὶ τοῦ Σωκράτους.

You and Plato were Socrates' students.
σὺ καὶ ὁ Πλάτων ἦστε μαθηταὶ τοῦ Σωκράτους.

3. Interestingly, a dual subject isn't necessarily accompanied by a dual verb; likewise a dual verb doesn't always have a grammatically dual subject.

Finally, in English, two singular subjects which are thought of as forming a unit or a whole can be construed with a singular verb:

Peanut butter and jelly is my favorite sandwich.

This phenomenon is only very rarely observed in Greek.

11.4 ASPECT AND TENSE

Consider the following series of sentences, arranged according to the conventional differentiation into six verb tenses:

Present: I believe what you say. [SIMPLE FACT IN THE PRESENT]

The neighbor's dog is barking [PROGRESSIVE ACTION IN THE PRESENT]

I walk the dog every morning. [REPEATED ACTION]

Love conquers all. [TIMELESS TRUTH]

I do love you. [EMPHATIC OR ONGOING]

Past: The ships sailed at dawn. [SIMPLE FACT IN THE PAST]

The Argonauts were sailing through the Hellespont. [PROGRESSIVE ACTION IN THE PAST]

We used to visit Delphi every summer. [REPEATED ACTION IN THE PAST]

I did love you. [PAST EMPHATIC OR ONGOING]

Future: We will leave for Troy tomorrow morning. [SIMPLE ACTION IN THE FUTURE]

We will be sailing all day. [PROGRESSIVE ACTION IN THE FUTURE]

I will walk the dog daily. [REPEATED ACTION IN THE FUTURE]

Present perfect: Socrates has arrived. (= Socrates is here)

I have learned Greek. (= I know Greek)

Past Perfect: By evening, Socrates had arrived. (= Socrates was there in the evening.)
By age twelve, I had learned Greek. (= I knew Greek at age twelve.)

Future Perfect: By this time tomorrow, Socrates will have arrived. (= Socrates will be here by this time tomorrow.)
By the time I am twenty, I will have learned Greek. (= I will know Greek when I am twenty.)

Although the word **tense** is derived from the Latin word *tempus*, meaning "time," it is clear that the distinction among these verbal phrases involves more than simple chronology. There are, after all, only three logical possibilities for the chronological relationship between an event or state of being and its being reported: prior (past), contemporaneous (present), and subsequent (future). There is another type of differentiation at work in these sentences, one that we will call **aspect**. What is indicated by the aspect of a verb form is not the time, relative to the speaker, that its action takes place but the type of action it is (ongoing, habitual, one-time, complete, or incomplete) and whether the speaker wishes to call attention to the action itself or to its result upon completion. Consequently, in addition to the three possible tenses, as narrowly defined chronologically, there are three possible aspects:

(1) The **imperfective** aspect specifies that an action is ongoing or habitual, and thus not completed (the name comes from the Latin word for "unfinished"). In the examples just above, the verbs in all of the sentences designated Present are imperfective in aspect, since none describes an action or state of being that has been completed. In general, present-tense verbs will be imperfective, since they are simultaneous with the reporting of them and hence must still be going on.[4] In the above sentences designated Past, the last three all

4. Some special cases might be seen as exceptions to this. In sentences containing a verb in the "historical present," the action is actually in the past although the verb tense is present (generally employed for enhanced liveliness), so the action may well be completed at the time of reporting ("so I stop at the library on the way home, and who do you think I see there . . ."). Other examples are jokes ("a guy walks into a bar with a penguin . . .") and narratives of hypothetical situations ("a man's son desperately needs a life-saving drug, but he can't afford to buy it, so he breaks into a pharmacy . . ."), where the present tense verb describes actions that are timeless, rather than simultaneous with their narration. Similarly, the present tense is often used in literary discussion to describe the actions of fictional characters ("in a fit of madness, Hamlet kills Polonius hiding behind the arras . . .").

relate uncompleted actions, since they describe situations as either ongoing ("were sailing") or repeated ("used to visit"). Thus their aspect is imperfective. Similarly, a sentence envisioning an ongoing, incomplete action in the future will contain a verb with imperfective aspect ("will be sailing").

(2) The **perfective** aspect, as you might expect (the name coming from the Latin word for "completed"), emphasizes the completion of the action, and the ongoing results—status rather than process. It can apply to actions in the present, past, or future, as noted in the examples above. In essence, the result that the speaker wants to call attention to will be one chronological step closer to the present than the action expressed by the verb. "Socrates has arrived" is a statement made about the present ("Socrates is here") by expressing a completed action in the past; hence the designation present perfect. So too, "Socrates had arrived" makes a statement about the past ("Socrates was there") with a verb whose action took place at an even earlier point in time.

(3) There remains one logical possibility: a verb expressing an action as a simple fact or event, with no reference to completeness or repetition. Here the traditional terminology employed in English syntax lets us down, and so we will anticipate the forthcoming discussion of the Greek verb and designate this third and final aspect as the **aoristic**. Since present tense verbs, for reasons given above, are almost always imperfective, the aoristic aspect is largely confined to verbs expressing past and future events. In the case of the former, such verbs are often said to be in the simple past, as opposed to the imperfective or perfective past. "The ships sailed at dawn" is an example of a sentence with an aoristic verb.

This system of tenses and aspects is fairly straightforward (not to say, rather elegant): three chronological tenses, each of which can theoretically be combined with three different aspects—nine possibilities. The situation only becomes muddled because the word "tense" is habitually used loosely to refer to both tense and aspect. This is true not only in descriptions of English syntax, where the term "aspect" is not even employed, but also in Greek, where it is. So the beginning student will learn that there are seven "tenses" for the Greek verb: present, imperfect, future, aorist, present perfect, past perfect (or pluperfect, as it is sometimes called), and future perfect. This taxonomy very closely approximates the English one delineated above and in fact conceals the same tense vs. aspect distinctions. The only difference is that whereas English uses auxiliary verbs to mark these distinctions, Greek employs inflectional affixation.

The imperfective aspect is found in the **present**, **imperfect**, and **future** tenses of the verb:

βαίνει πρὸς τὴν ἀγοράν. He is going to the market. *or* He goes to the market.

ἔβαινε πρὸς τὴν ἀγοράν. He was going to the market. *or* He used to go to the market.

βήσεται πρὸς τὴν ἀγοράν. He will be going to the market. *or* He will go to the market.

The perfective aspect finds expression in the **perfect**, **pluperfect**, and **future perfect** tenses:

βέβηκε πρὸς τὴν ἀγοράν. He has gone to the market.

ἐβεβήκει πρὸς τὴν ἀγοράν. He had gone to the market.

βεβηκὼς ἔσται πρὸς τὴν ἀγοράν. He will have gone to the market.

The aoristic aspect is found in a past tense that is appropriately, but confusingly, named the **aorist** "tense." Some actions in the future might also be considered aoristic in aspect, in which case the future tense is employed, making no distinction with the imperfective future. Similarly, in those special cases (see comment #5 below) where the present tense is used for past events, the present tense verb form can have an aoristic aspect.

ἔβη πρὸς τὴν ἀγοράν. He went to the market.

βήσεται πρὸς τὴν ἀγοράν. He will go to the market.

βαίνει πρὸς τὴν ἀγοράν. He goes (i.e., went) to the market.

The following table shows how these temporal and aspectual possibilities are combined in the seven Greek tenses (designated in upper case):

	Imperfective	Aoristic	Perfective
Present	PRESENT	PRESENT	PERFECT
Past	IMPERFECT	AORIST	PLUPERFECT
Future	FUTURE	FUTURE	FUTURE PERFECT

Or, to present the same information with a different orientation:

GREEK TENSES	POTENTIAL ASPECTS
Present	Imperfective or Aoristic
Future	Imperfective or Aoristic
Imperfect	Imperfective
Aorist	Aoristic
Perfect	Perfective
Pluperfect	Perfective
Future Perfect	Perfective

Some things to note:

(1) The non-past tenses—the present, perfect, future, and future perfect—are called the **primary tenses**; and the imperfect, aorist, and pluperfect tenses are called the **secondary tenses.** This distinction will become relevant in the syntax of subordinate clauses, where a sentence whose main clause contains a verb in a primary tense will be said to constitute a **primary sequence**, and a sentence whose main verb is in a secondary tense will be said to constitute a **secondary sequence**. Note that the secondary tenses—the true "past" tenses—are marked in the indicative mood by the **temporal augment** which is prefixed to the verb form: ἔ-βαινε, ἔ-βη, ἐ-βεβήκει. It is important to remember that *it is the augment that marks these forms as true past-tense forms, not the stem.*

(2) So although the aorist form of a verb that appears in the list of that verb's principal parts is indicative, and thus a true past-tense form, you should not think of the term "aorist" itself as being equivalent to "past." "Aorist" refers to *aspect*, as defined above, rather than time, and is in fact non-temporal in all forms that lack the temporal augment: the non-indicative moods (imperative, optative, and subjunctive) and the deverbatives (participles and infinitives).

(3) Similarly, the common shortening of "present perfect" to "perfect" when referring to this principal part of a verb conceals the fact that the perfect is felt to be a true present tense, in spite of the fact that the action it describes took place in the past. This is evidenced inflectionally—by the fact that the perfect form lacks the augment—as well as syntactically in the rules for primary and secondary sequences, where the perfect is treated as a primary tense.

(4) It is particularly important to understand clearly the difference between the imperfect and aorist tenses when talking about the past. The imperfect is used for the description of circumstances, for general information, for habitual or ongoing actions, or for the endeavor (perhaps ultimately unsuccessful) to perform an action. The aorist is employed for the factual statement of actions that are discrete events, successfully completed. For example: "Once upon a time there was a kingdom ruled by a wise and kindly king who had a beautiful daughter. She was so beautiful that young men from miles around repeatedly came and sought her hand in marriage. Then one day a mysterious stranger rode up to the castle and asked to speak with the king . . ." All of the underlined verbs in the first two sentences would be in the imperfect tense, those in the last sentence in the aorist.

(5) There are instances in which the tenses are used seemingly in violation of their chronological sense. As in the English examples provided in footnote 4, above, Greek offers a historical present, to increase the drama or liveliness of a narrative. The present is also on occasion used for future events, to stress the immediacy or certainty of their occurrence. The aorist is often used in place of the present in statements of general truth, a use designated as the **gnomic aorist**. Similes have much the same timeless quality as do proverbs, and here too the aorist is sometimes employed (mostly in poetry) where the present or imperfect might be expected. In the **epistolary aorist**, the writer of a letter adopts the chronological standpoint of the reader in the future and uses the aorist tense instead of the present to describe circumstances pertaining to the time of writing.

11.5 VOICE

The grammatical characteristic of **voice** expresses an important concept for verbs. Since verbs typically involve the notion of action, voice addresses the issues of where the action of the verb originates and where it ends. In some constructions, an action originates from the grammatical subject. In others, the action ends at the grammatical subject. And in still others, the action both originates and ends at the subject. These differences in "verbal trajectory" are crucial for understanding the concept of voice.

There are three different voices in Greek: active, middle, and passive. They are usually distinguished by means of inflectional endings.

In an **active** construction, the action simply originates outward from the subject:

We looked. ἐβλέψαμεν.

They will stop the enemy. τοὺς πολεμίους παύσουσιν.

In a **middle** construction, the action originates from the subject but then in some way boomerangs back to the subject. Thus, the subject is acting on or for itself:

We looked (for ourselves). ἐβλεψάμεθα.

They will stop (themselves). παύσονται.

In **passive** constructions, the action of the verb acts on the subject. Thus, the subject receives the verb's action, which has originated elsewhere:

We were looked at. ἐβλέφθημεν.

They will be stopped by the enemy. παυθήσονται ὑπὸ τῶν πολεμίων.

The active and passive voices are familiar enough to English speakers. You may have even had the experience of being instructed not to use the passive voice in your writing. True, a passive constructive may lack specificity, but an artful writer, at well chosen moments, can intend to be somewhat vague.

In English, we can express middle-voice concepts with the use of reflexive pronouns:

He looked <u>at himself</u> in the mirror.

They will enjoy <u>themselves</u> skiing.

Notice how if the preceding reflexives had been omitted, the sense of the sentences wouldn't be much affected.

Sometimes a middle idea can be inherent in certain verbs. For example, when you're told, "Wash before dinner!," you know to wash *yourself*. If a headline reads, "America Defends against Terrorism," you know that America is defending *itself*.

Finally, English can use a construction with the auxiliary verb "get" to express the idea of the middle voice (that is, a verbal trajectory medial between the active and passive voices):

Jill got herself promoted.

Those guys got themselves caught in a sting operation.

Notice the semantic differences between the preceding examples and their passive and active counterparts:

Jill was promoted.

The boss promoted Jill.

Those guys were caught in a sting operation.

A sting operation caught those guys.

You can see how in the middle construction the subjects are implied to play a greater role in the actions of being promoted or being caught than the active and passive constructions convey.

Back to Greek again: the inflectional forms of active verbs are unique; the inflectional forms of the middle and the passive are identical in all tenses except the future and aorist tenses, where the passive voice employs distinctive infixes.

Greek active and middle verbs may or may not take a direct object; passive verbs do not.[5] Often the difference between middle verbs and active verbs which employ reflexive or reciprocal pronouns is extremely nuanced and can't easily be discerned. Sometimes this difference is merely one of authorial preference and has, therefore, no real semantic significance.

Certain Greek verbs occur *only* in the middle and passive forms in all tenses; when found with middle forms, these verbs seem to have an active sense and

5. The only exception to this rule is verbs which take double accusative direct objects (e.g., the verbs "to teach," "to ask," "to persuade of," "to deprive of"), where one object is a person and the other a thing. When such a verb is used in the passive voice, the person is changed into the nominative case, while the accusative is retained for the thing:
ἐδίδασκον ἡμᾶς ταύτην τὴν τέχνην: they were teaching us this skill
ἡμεῖς ἐδιδασκόμεθα ταύτην τὴν τέχνην: we were being taught this skill

no discernible middle force at all. These verbs are called **deponent verbs**, and it isn't really evident by their usage that their meaning implies reflexivity or self-benefit (the hallmark features of the middle voice); rather, they seem to be active in everything but form. Deponents often—but not exclusively—pertain to physical activities (ἅλλομαι "jump"; πέτομαι "fly"; ὀρχέομαι "dance"; δέρκομαι "glower") or cognition (οἴομαι "think"; βούλομαι "want"; αἰσθάνομαι "perceive"; ἡγέομαι "consider"). The existence of deponent verbs may be a vestige of the Indo-European parent language, while many of the verbs themselves that became deponents probably did so only as a matter of development and popular usage.

For a small class of verbs, the middle and passive forms are employed exclusively in particular tenses, while in other tenses forms of the active voice can be found. These verbs are sometimes referred to as **semi-deponents**. If their forms are active in the present system and middle in the future system, they use passive forms in the aoristic system; these passives may be more middle (e.g., reflexive) in meaning, and a direct object can even be allowed with them (which is atypical of true passives).

Deponents and semi-deponents, because they're lacking some forms, will have distinctive principal parts. Exercise special care in learning them. Deponents' dictionary entries always list them under their present middle/passive form.

11.5.1 FINE POINTS

Now that you understand the general characteristics of voice, you're prepared to be initiated into some of the finer points of Greek voice.

With respect to the characteristic of voice, Greek active verbs can be transitive or intransitive; Greek middles, similarly, can be transitive or intransitive; Greek passives are usually intransitive but can be found used transitively more often than English passives.

Some Greek verbs have a common meaning in the active voice and a different and distinct meaning in the middle voice. One voice (usually the active) is typically transitive, while the other voice (usually the middle) is intransitive. The transitive verb usually retains the passive in all tenses, but the intransitive may also share the distinctive passives in the future and aorist. You'll note that the middle voice frequently connotes greater deliberateness or intention than its active counterpart. Since these verbs often cause beginning students problems, it would be helpful to master this list of the more common ones:

αἱρέω: take	αἱρέομαι: choose
ἅπτω: attach	ἅπτομαι: touch
ἄρχω: start	ἄρχομαι: initiate, lead
γράφω: write	γράφομαι: draft, draw up
ἔχω: hold	ἔχομαι: clutch, cling to
πείθω: persuade	πείθομαι: obey
τίνω: pay	τίνομαι: exact
φυλάττω: guard	φυλάττομαι: be on guard against
χράω: lend	χράομαι: apply, put to use

For those Greek verbs which have both a 1st (weak) aorist and a 2nd (strong) aorist and/or a 1st perfect and a 2nd perfect, usually the 1st's are transitive and the 2nd's are intransitive.

For most Greek verbs, the passive forms represent the passive of the active; sometimes passive forms represent the passive of both the active and the middle (even when the meanings of the active and middle differ, as we saw above); and sometimes the passive forms represent the passive of only the middle (preserving some middle force). In fine, the semantic range and coverage of a given verb's passive forms is a matter of some common usage and isn't really predictable.

Finally, it's worth noting that Greek, like English, exhibits a certain avoidance of the passive voice. Some common active and deponent verbs are employed in preference to the use of passives. E.g.,

ἁλίσκομαι, "be caught," is preferred to the passive of αἱρέω, "catch" or "take"

ἀποθνῄσκω, "die," is preferred to the passive of ἀποκτείνω, "kill"

γίγνομαι, "be born," is preferred to the passive of τίκτω, "give birth to"

κεῖμαι, "lie," is preferred to the passive of τίθημι, "lay out"

πάσχω, "suffer," is preferred to the passive of ποιέω, "do"

πίπτω, "fall," is preferred to the passive of βάλλω, "hit"

φεύγω, "flee," is preferred to the passive of διώκω, "chase"

In sum, the basic problem students of beginning Greek have with the notion of middle verbs is this: their semantics are rather unpredictable! Should they be translated to reflect self-benefit? reflexivity? neither? The short (albeit unhelpful) answer is "Yes!" Some Greek middles can and do reflect self-benefit; some don't. Some can and do convey an explicit or implicit reflexivity; some don't. And still others are middle verbs for no obvious or arguable reason. The best procedure to follow is to take careful note of a verb when it's used distinctively in the middle. This way, you'll broaden your Greek vocabulary at the same time as you deepen your appreciation for Greek idiom and nuance.

11.6 NEGATION

An English declarative sentence is most simply negated with the adverb "not." The syntax of negation differs, however, depending on whether or not there is an auxiliary in the sentence.

If an auxiliary verb is present, the negating adverb is placed directly after it:

The ship is departing.

The ship is <u>not</u> departing.

We will go to the theater tonight.

We will <u>not</u> go to the theater tonight.

I have seen that play before.

I have <u>not</u> seen that play before.

If the sentence contains a simple verb, it is the emphatic form of the sentence that is negated, with the auxiliary verb "do":

I see what you mean. → I <u>do</u> see what you mean. → I <u>do</u> <u>not</u> see what you mean.

The speaker persuaded the jury. → The speaker <u>did</u> persuade the jury. → The speaker <u>did</u> <u>not</u> persuade the jury.

When you are translating such a negated sentence into Greek, it is important to remember that there will be no word in the Greek corresponding to the English "do" or "did."

In addition to the adverb "not," English can alternatively express negation through the use of other negative adverbs and pronouns, such as "nobody," "nowhere," "never," etc. The key word here is *alternatively*: in a given sentence one or the other negative may be used, but not both (which results in the colloquialism known as the double negative):

I do not trust anybody in that family.

or

I trust nobody in that family.

This plan is not going anywhere.

or

This plan is going nowhere.

If on occasion a double negative is intentionally used, the negatives cancel each other, resulting in a positive statement.

We can't just do nothing. [I.e., we must do something.]

The negation of imperatives follows the same rule as that of sentences with simple verbs. It is the strengthened form of the imperative, with the auxiliary "do," that is negated:

Tell the children this story. → Do tell the children this story. → Do not tell the children this story.

Here again, there will be no word in Greek prohibitions corresponding to the English "do."

Greek possesses two simple negating adverbs, οὐ (sometimes appearing as οὐκ or οὐχ) and μή. They are usually placed directly before the verb that they negate.

τὸ πλοῖον ἀπέρχεται.

τὸ πλοῖον οὐκ ἀπέρχεται.

λέγε τόνδε τὸν λόγον τοῖς παισίν.

μὴ εἴπῃς τόνδε τὸν λόγον τοῖς παισίν.

Generally, οὐ is used to negate factual assertions with verbs in the indicative mood. Imperatives and subjunctives are generally negated with μή. Optatives, participles, and infinitives may require either one, depending on the syntactic situation. The appropriate choice of negative in each case will be noted as each of these constructions is discussed below.

Like English, Greek also has a full range of other negative adverbs and pronouns. Each is a compound of either οὐ or μή and is used in the same syntactic situations where the simple οὐ or μή would be used:

οὐδεὶς φιλεῖ τὸν τύραννον.

No one loves the tyrant.

μήποτε πειθώμεθα ἐκείνῳ τῷ κακῷ ἀνθρώπῳ.

Let us never obey that evil man.

In contrast to English, double negatives in Greek sentences are grammatically acceptable, and depending on the type and order of the negatives, can serve either to enhance or cancel out the negativity. If a negative compound precedes a simple negative, the result is a positive statement:

οὐδὲν οὐκ εἶδον.

I saw something. [Literally: I didn't see nothing.]

But if a negative compound follows a simple negative or another compound, the negativity is reinforced:

οὐδεὶς οὐδὲν ἐν τῷ σκότῳ εἶδεν.

No one saw anything at all in the darkness.

With certain verbs, particularly verbs of speaking or thinking, the negative οὐ does not negate the meaning of the verb but gives it the *opposite* meaning:

οὐκ ἔφην τὸν Σωκράτην σοφώτατον εἶναι.

This sentence does not mean "I did not assert that Socrates is the wisest" but rather "I denied that Socrates is the wisest," which is a much stronger statement.

11.7 MOOD

The **mood** of a verb form reflects the way in which the speaker wants the action or condition expressed by the verb to be understood. In English, there are three verbal moods: the indicative, imperative, and subjunctive.

An **indicative** verb form expresses an action or circumstance as a factual assertion:

The Spartans are preparing for battle.

Plato was a student of Socrates.

We will offer a sacrifice to the gods tomorrow.

Note that the assertion does not have to be true, but merely expressed in the form of a fact: the sentence "Plato was a student of Confucius" would also require a verb in the indicative mood, even though its assertion is false. Indicative sentences such as these are called **declarative** sentences. The indicative is also used in **interrogative** sentences, where the speaker is asking whether a factual assertion is true, or is seeking other kinds of information about it:

Are the Spartans preparing for war?

When was Plato a student of Socrates?

Why will we offer a sacrifice to the gods tomorrow?

As its name suggests, the **imperative** mood is employed when the verb is a command or a direct request:

Announce this news to the assembly.

Please pass the salt.

These are **2nd-person imperatives**. The implied subject of such verbs is the person or persons being addressed by the speaker: if it is one person, the subject is 2nd-person singular; if it's more than one, it is 2nd-person plural. English makes no morphological distinction between the two.

There are situations where the speaker expresses an order to be carried out by a person or persons other than those he is addressing, essentially a **3rd-person imperative**. English most commonly uses auxiliary verbs for this:

Have the soldiers arrest anyone who looks suspicious.

I'm busy. Let John do it.

Regarding the second example, it is important not to confuse this use of "let" with that which means "permit" or "allow." The sense here is not that John is to be *allowed* to do it but that he be *ordered* or *required* to do it: an alternative expression would be "Tell John to do it."

This word "let" is also employed in a construction that might be considered a 1st-person imperative, although it is conventionally characterized as **hortatory**:

What shall I do? Let me see.

Let's (= let us) meet tomorrow at noon.

The **subjunctive** mood was once more prevalent in English than it is today, having been largely replaced by the indicative. With the subjunctive the speaker expresses that the action or state expressed by the verb is not factual but instead hypothetical, potential, wished for, or conditional. The only remaining distinct subjunctive inflectional form in English is the 3rd-person singular of the present tense, where the *-(e)s* suffix of the indicative is omitted:

Indicative: A good orator speaks clearly.

Subjunctive: It is necessary that a good orator speak clearly.

For the verb *to be*, the subjunctive forms in English are "be" and "were":

Be that as it may, I still think you are wrong.

Don't look at me as if I were crazy.

There are a few syntactic constructions in which the subjunctive is still employed in formal contemporary English:

(1) In subordinate clauses after verbs or phrases that express commands, necessity, requests, suggestions, etc.

The council insisted that he undergo questioning.

The gods demand that sacrifices be pure.

(2) In the expression of wishes, often in combination with the words "may" (for possible wishes) or "would that" (for impossible wishes):

May she rest in peace.

Would that it were true.

(3) In conditional sentences, to express conditions that are either somewhat doubtful or completely contrafactual:

Were he to do this, what would be his reward? (were he to = if he should)

If I were you, I would be careful.

(4) In object clauses with verbs of fearing, after the archaic word "lest":

I fear lest your dire prediction come true.

The Greek verb has four moods: indicative, imperative, subjunctive, and optative. With very few exceptions, they are all inflectionally distinct from one another. The aorist imperative, subjunctive, and optative forms lack the augment and thus have no temporal significance. The difference between these forms and their present-tense and perfect-tense equivalents is purely one of aspect (see §11.4).

11.7.1 Indicative: the Greek **indicative** mood has largely the same significance as its English counterpart, marking a statement as a factual assertion or a question of fact:

οἱ δοῦλοι ἐργάζονται ἐν τοῖς ἀγροῖς.
The slaves are working in the fields.

ὁ Θησεὺς ἀπέκτεινε τὸν Μινόταυρον.
Theseus killed the Minotaur.

τίς τοῦτο τῷ πατρὶ λέξει;
Who will tell my father this?

διὰ τί ἐλήλυθας;
Why have you come?

11.7.2 Imperative: the Greek **imperative** mood differs from the English in that not only are the forms for singular and plural inflectionally distinct, but there are 3rd-person as well as 2nd-person forms. There are imperative forms in the present, aorist, and (more rarely) the perfect tenses.

τίμα τὴν μητέρα σου καὶ τὸν πατέρα.
Honor your mother and father.

φιλεῖτε τὸν γείτονά σου.
Love your neighbor.

γραφόντων οἱ μαθηταὶ ἐπιστολὴν τῷ διδασκάλῳ.
Have the students write a letter to their teacher.

πεποιηκὼς ἴσθι τοῦτο δι᾽ ὀλίγου.
Finish this soon. (Literally: Have done this soon.)

11.7.3 Subjunctive: verbs in the **subjunctive** mood always refer to future events or states that are potential or indeterminate, rather than those that the speaker feels to be certain (to the extent that the future is ever certain), for which the future indicative is employed. Subjunctive forms are found in the present, aorist, and perfect tenses.

There are a few situations in which the verb of the main clause will be in the subjunctive mood:

(1) The **hortatory** subjunctive, in the 1st-person plural, is the Greek equivalent of the "let us" construction in English:

μαχώμεθα μεγάλῳ θάρσῳ.
Let us fight with great valor.

(2) Also occurring only in the 1st person, singular or plural, is the **deliberative** subjunctive. It expresses a greater uncertainty than usual on the part of the speaker about what he will or should do, or else it serves as a purely rhetorical question not necessarily requiring an answer:

τί εἴπω τοῖς δικασταῖς;
What am I to say to the jury?

μαχώμεθα ἢ φεύγωμεν;
Are we to fight or flee?

τί νομίσω;
What am I to think?

(3) The subjunctive is regularly used in **prohibitions** (i.e., negative commands), usually in the aorist tense:

μὴ πιστεύσῃς τοῖς πολεμίοις.
Don't trust the enemy.

Most commonly, the subjunctive mood is used with verbs in subordinate clauses.

Purpose clauses (§20) express the purpose for which the action in the main verb was performed:

φυλάττουσι τὰς πύλας ἵνα τὸν κλῶπα λάβωσιν.
They are guarding the gates in order to catch the thief.

Clauses of fearing (§22.2) are used with verbs expressing fear to denote the object of the fear:

φοβοῦμαι μὴ ὁ Κύκλωψ ἡμᾶς φάγῃ.
I fear that the Cyclops will eat us.

Conditional (§17.2), relative (§19), and temporal (§24) clauses can be **generalized** by putting their verbs into the subjunctive—the equivalent of adding the suffix *-ever* in English, as in whoever, whenever, if ever, etc.:

ὅστις ἂν πλοῦτον ἔχῃ, πολλοὺς φίλους ἔχει.
Whoever has wealth has many friends.

ὅταν λέγῃ ὁ Περικλῆς, ὁ δῆμος ἀκούει.
Whenever Pericles speaks, the people listen.

ἐὰν ὁ Μίλων ἀγωνίζηται, νικᾷ.
If (ever) Milo competes, he wins.

Finally, the subjunctive is employed in the protasis (the if-clause) of certain future conditional sentences (to be discussed as **future more vivid**, §17.3) where the speaker feels relatively certain that the condition will come to pass:

ἐὰν ἀνδρείως μαχώμεθα, ἡ πόλις ἡμᾶς ἀεὶ τιμήσει.
If we fight bravely, the city will honor us forever.

11.7.4 Optative: like the subjunctive, the **optative** mood is also used in both independent and subordinate clauses. Optative forms are found in the present, aorist, perfect, and future tenses. There are two chief uses in independent clauses.

The optative can be used to express a **wish** (hence its name), on the speaker's part, that something take place. It can be used alone or in conjunction with the particles εἴθε or εἰ γάρ:

σῴζοιεν οἱ θεοὶ τὴν βασίλειαν.
May the gods save the queen.

μήποτε μανθάνοις τὴν ἀλήθειαν.
May you never learn the truth.

εἴθε ὁ ἄριστος νικῴη.
May the best man win.

It is, of course, much more idiomatic in contemporary English to introduce such optatives with a phrase like "I wish that," "I hope that," or "if only." Note that this optative construction is only used for wishes that have the potential to be fulfilled.[6]

The other important use of the optative in independent clauses is referred to as the **potential** optative. It expresses a verbal action as potential rather than certain and is often used to weaken or soften an indicative assertion or a command for the sake of politeness or deference. It is accompanied by the particle ἄν:

βουλοίμην ἂν γαμεῖν τὴν θυγατέρα σου.
I would like to marry your daughter. [As opposed to, "I want. . . ."]

6. For impossible wishes, the verb will be in the imperfect indicative, for reasons to be explained below (§17.4):
εἰ γὰρ μήποτε ἐγενόμην.
If only I had never been born.

εἴποις ἄν μοι τὸ ὄνομα σοῦ;

Would you tell me your name? [As opposed to, "Tell me. . . ."]

Most other uses of the optative occur in subordinate clauses. It commonly substitutes for the subjunctive when the verb in the main clause is in a secondary tense. The past-tense equivalents of the examples of subjunctive usage listed above would be as follows:

Purpose clause: ἐφύλαττον τὰς πύλας ἵνα τὸν κλῶπα λάβοιεν.

They were guarding the gates in order to catch the thief.

Clause of fearing: ἐφοβούμην μὴ ὁ Κύκλωψ ἡμᾶς φάγοι.

I feared that the Cyclopes would eat us.

Generalizing clauses: ὅστις πλοῦτον ἔχοι, πολλοὺς φίλους εἶχεν.

Whoever had wealth, had many friends.

ὅτε λέγοι ὁ Περικλῆς, ὁ δῆμος ἤκουεν.

Whenever Pericles would speak, the people listened.

εἰ ὁ Μίλων ἀγωνίζοιτο, ἐνίκα.

If (ever) Milo would compete, he won.

The optative is used in both clauses of so-called **future-less-vivid** conditions (see §17.3), where there is greater doubt that the condition will be fulfilled:

εἰ ἀνδρείως μαχοίμεθα, ἡ πόλις ἡμᾶς ἂν ἀεὶ τιμῴη.

If we were to fight bravely, the city would honor us forever.

Finally, the optative substitutes for the indicative in certain situations in indirect statement, after a past-tense main verb. These will be taken up in §16.4.

12. INFINITIVES

The conjugated verb forms discussed to this point are designated as **finite** forms of the verb. Each form shows (i.e., is bounded by) person, number, voice, tense, and mood, and each form can function as the verb of either an independent or subordinate clause. By contrast, the **infinitive** (from the Latin word for "unbounded") forms of a verb function most often as verbal nouns, and show only tense/aspect and voice.

In English, the infinitive is a phrase, comprising the word "to" along with the verb and, in some cases, modal auxiliaries. Transitive English verbs have four infinitives, active and passive, in the present and perfect:

present active: to see

perfect active: to have seen

present passive: to be seen

perfect passive: to have been seen

As noun phrases, infinitives can function as subjects or predicate nouns:

To desire happiness surpasses all human impulses.

To be obeyed by the people is more important than to be loved by them.

Never to have seen Athens is never to have lived.

As these examples show, the verbal nature of the infinitive allows it to govern direct objects as well as to be modified by adverbs and prepositional phrases.

English infinitives can also be used as the objects of verbs, in which function they are often labeled **complementary** infinitives:

I want to know the truth.

I hope to see you soon.

I would hate to miss the show.

In these examples, the implied subject of the infinitive is the same as the subject of the main verb. When this is not the case, and where the subject of the infinitive is expressed by a personal pronoun, it must be in the objective (i.e., accusative) case:

I want them to know the truth.

I would hate for her to miss the show.

Note that the infinitive construction cannot always be maintained when the subject differs from that of the main verb. For the second example above, one would have to substitute a subordinate clause for the infinitive, and its subject would be in the nominative case:

I hope that we see you soon.

Beyond functioning as the subject and object of verbs, infinitives appear in English in a wide variety of contexts. They are often used with adjectives to limit or define the sense in which the adjective applies, as in phrases such as "happy to see you" or "eager to return." Infinitives play the same role with certain nouns, for example, "the right to speak" or "the desire to eat."

An alternative to the future tense employing the modal "will" is the use of the infinitive after the participle "going":

I will set out in the morning.

I am going to set out in the morning.

Infinitives are commonly used to express the purpose for which the action in the main verb is undertaken, but only when the subject of the verb and the infinitive are the same:

They sailed to Salamis to escape the Persians.

but

They sailed to Salamis so that the Persians would not capture them.

Certain verbs expressing mental or verbal activity can take an infinitive phrase as an alternative to a subordinate clause introduced by the conjunction "that." Here again, pronominal subjects of the infinitive must be in the objective case:

I believe that he is a fool.

I believe him to be a fool.

The assembly declared that they were public enemies.

The assembly declared them to be public enemies.

A Greek verb can have as many as eleven infinitive forms, corresponding to all combinations of the three voices and seven tenses, with the exception of the imperfect and pluperfect tenses. Note that the different "tenses" of the infinitive reflect aspectual rather than temporal distinctions:

present active: γράφειν to write

present middle/passive: γράφεσθαι to write (for oneself)/to be written

future active: γράψειν to write, to be going to write

future middle: γράψεσθαι to write (for oneself), to be going to write (for oneself)

future passive: γραφήσεσθαι to be written, to be going to be written

aorist active: γράψαι to write

aorist middle: γράψασθαι to write (for oneself)

aorist passive: γραφῆναι to be written

perfect active: γεγραφέναι to have written

perfect middle/passive: γεγράφθαι to have written (for oneself)/to have been written

future perfect middle/passive: γεγράφεσθαι to have been going to be written (for oneself)/to have been about to be written

Many of the uses of the infinitive in Greek overlap those in English. The complementary infinitive functions as the object of the main verb:

βούλομαι εἰπεῖν σοί.

I want to talk to you.

ἐκέλευσεν ἡμᾶς μένειν ἐν τῷ πλοίῳ

He commanded us to remain on the ship.

If expressed, the subject of the infinitive is in the accusative case, unless it is the same as the subject of the main verb, in which case although it is unexpected it is in the nominative:

βούλομαι σὲ εἰπεῖν ἐμοί.

I want you to talk to me.

βούλομαι εἶναι πλούσιος.

I want to be rich.

Precisely because the infinitive lacks a personal subject, it commonly occurs in impersonal constructions:

> δεῖ μαθεῖν τὴν ἀλήθειαν.
>
> It is necessary to learn the truth.

> πρέπει τιμᾶν τοὺς δικαίους.
>
> It is proper to honor the just.

> χαλεπόν ἐστι φιλεῖν τοὺς πολεμίους.
>
> It is difficult to love one's enemies.

With few exceptions, infinitives are negated with μή:

> ἐκέλευσεν ἡμᾶς μὴ μένειν ἐν τῷ πλοίῳ.
>
> He commanded us not to remain on the ship.

> χαλεπόν ἐστι μὴ φιλεῖν τοῦτον τὸν ἄνδρα.
>
> It is difficult not to love this man.

Certain adjectives have their meaning refined or limited by the addition of infinitive phrases, as they do in English:

> οὗτος ὁ νεανίας ἄξιός ἐστι γαμεῖν τὴν θυγατέρα μου.
>
> This young man is worthy to marry my daughter.

The infinitive regularly occurs in result clauses, when the result is envisioned as potential rather than reported as actual (see §21):

> ἡ Ἀταλάντη οὕτω ταχέως τρέχει ὥστε οὐδένα αὐτὴν νικᾶν.
>
> Atalanta runs so swiftly that no one would defeat her.

That the infinitive is grammatically a singular neuter noun is made clear by the construction known as the **articular infinitive**, where the infinitive is preceded by a neuter definite article that acts as a case indicator. It often functions as a substitute for the gerund that is lacking in Greek:

> πολλὰ διδάσκομεν τῷ παιδεύειν.
>
> We learn much by teaching.

> τοῦ γιγνώσκειν ἕνεκα ἀκούουσιν.

ὑπὲρ τοῦ γιγνώσκειν ἀκούουσιν.

They listen in order to understand.

διὰ τὸ τὰς γυναῖκας τὴν ἀκρόπολιν ᾑρηκέναι, οἱ ἄνδρες παύουσι τὸν πόλεμον.

Because of the women having captured the citadel, the men are stopping the war.

Note again that the subject of the preceding articular infinitive was placed in the accusative case (τὰς γυναῖκας).

A small number of verbs allow an absolute infinitive construction (see §14.3), which can sometimes be literally translated with an English infinitive and sometimes not:

ὡς ἔπος εἰπεῖν . . .	so to speak . . .
ὡς ἐμοὶ δοκεῖν . . .	as it seems to me . . .

The infinitive can be used in place of the imperative, more often in poetry than prose:

μὴ φοβεῖσθαι.

Don't be afraid.

Not to fear!

The infinitive is also commonly used in indirect statement, as discussed in §16.2.

13. PARTICIPLES

The most common deverbative adjectives are called **participles**. English participles exhibit neither variety nor much frequency. Greek participles, on the other hand, are many and richly varied in their settings and senses. Indeed, it's often said that no good Greek sentence lacks a participle. While that may be an overstatement, it is, in fact, popular sport among Greek students to count participles—it's not hard to find sentences with five or six participles!

English has two natural participles: a present active and a perfect passive:

the praising poet

the praised athlete

The present active participle always has the *-ing* suffix,[1] while the perfect passive usually exhibits the *-(e)d* suffix, though the *-(e)n* suffix (e.g., spoken, taken, known, proven) is also quite common. Other types of perfect passive participles, especially of Germanic origin, can also be found (e.g., met, taught, brought, sung, gone, swum). These irregulars are usually found as the third principal part of verb entries in unabridged English dictionaries.

Other English participles are created periphrastically (that is, with the verb *to be* expressed or implied) to imitate the richer array of classical participles, but they often seem formal or even awkward:

the poet having praised [perfect active]

the athlete about to be praised [future passive]

Greek participles can be found in five tenses (present, future, aorist, perfect, and future perfect) and in all three voices (active, middle, and passive). Moreover, the aoristic aspect is operative in all aorist participles, just as the imperfective aspect obtains for all present participles. The primary reason, then, why Greek participles are more frequent than English: there are up to fourteen of them for the normal verb, compared with just two in English. So

1. Exercise care in distinguishing the *-ing* suffix used both in gerunds and in present participles in English:
smoking is unhealthy [GERUND]
the smoking gun [PARTICIPLE].

the nominative masculine singular participles for the Greek verb παύω, for example, are:

	ACTIVE	MIDDLE	PASSIVE
PRESENT	παύων	παυόμενος	παυόμενος
FUTURE	παύσων	παυσόμενος	παυσθησόμενος
AORIST	παύσας	παυσάμενος	παυσθείς
PERFECT	πεπαυκώς	πεπαυμένος	πεπαυμένος
FUTURE PERFECT		πεπαυσόμενος	πεπαυσόμενος[2]

Translated, these mean:

	ACTIVE	MIDDLE	PASSIVE
PRESENT	stopping	stopping (oneself)	being stopped
FUTURE	about to stop	about to stop (oneself)	about to be stopped
AORIST	stopping	stopping (oneself)	(being) stopped
PERFECT	having stopped	having stopped (oneself)	(having been) stopped
FUTURE PERFECT		about to have stopped (oneself)	about to have been stopped

Remember: the present participles have an imperfective aspect, while the aorist participles have an aoristic aspect.

As adjectives, Greek participles display the characteristics of case, number, and gender so that they properly agree with the nouns or pronouns they modify:

τὸ ποίημα τοῦ ἐπαινοῦντος ποιητοῦ: the poem of the praising poet

τῷ ἐπαινηθέντι ποιητῇ: to/for the praised poet

Sometimes the adjectival qualities and sometimes the verbal qualities are emphasized for participles, being verbal adjectives. For example, the phrase "the running man" tells you *what kind of* man is referred to: a *running* man.

2. The future perfect participles are quite rare. The active would be expressed periphrastically (πεπαυκὼς ἐσόμενος: about to have been stopping), if at all; the passive is more common than the middle, but infrequent nonetheless.

Thus, the adjectival force of the participle is here foremost. When English wants to feature the verbal qualities of a participle, the syntax is altered somewhat: the man *running* into the shrine (not the running-into-the-shrine man). This phrase doesn't really describe the man so much as what he's doing (i.e., running into the shrine).

Greek also clearly distinguishes between the adjectival and the verbal force of its participles. When functioning like an attributive adjective, the Greek participle is typically placed between the definite article and the substantive, or after the article and noun with a repetition of the article:

ὁ ἐπαινῶν ποιητής

or

ὁ ποιητὴς ὁ ἐπαινῶν

the praising poet[3]

When the participle functions predicatively (which is its most common usage in Greek), neither is it placed between the substantive and its article nor does it require a repetition of the article; rather, it can be found virtually anywhere else in its sentence or clause:

ἐπαινῶν ὁ ποιητὴς ἀείδει

or

ὁ ποιητὴς ἐπαινῶν ἀείδει

or

ὁ ποιητὴς ἀείδει ἐπαινῶν

the poet sings, praising . . .

If the participial phrases above are to be expanded with, for example, the object "the city," Greek word order remains fairly flexible:

ὁ ἐπαινῶν ποιητὴς τὴν πόλιν

or

ὁ ἐπαινῶν τὴν πόλιν ποιητής

or

3. A third option, quite rare, allows ποιητὴς ὁ ἐπαινῶν ("the praising poet").

ὁ τὴν πόλιν ἐπαινῶν ποιητής

or even

ποιητὴς ὁ τὴν πόλιν ἐπαινῶν

the poet praising the city

τὴν πόλιν ἐπαινῶν ὁ ποιητὴς ἀείδει

or

ὁ ποιητὴς τὴν πόλιν ἐπαινῶν ἀείδει

or

ὁ ποιητὴς ἀείδει τὴν πόλιν ἐπαινῶν

or

ἐπαινῶν τὴν πόλιν ὁ ποιητὴς ἀείδει

or

ὁ ποιητὴς ἐπαινῶν τὴν πόλιν ἀείδει

or

ὁ ποιητὴς ἀείδει ἐπαινῶν τὴν πόλιν

the poet sings, praising the city

The characteristic observed just above is probably the greatest reason—apart from the alphabet—why Greek seems so foreign to English speakers. Again, smart students of Greek need to break themselves of the English habit of reading from left to right; the usage of Greek participles often requires students to (temporarily) read from right to left or inside out!

Another reason Greek participles are so common is because they have a broader semantic range than English participles. "The running man" has a fairly restricted sense; but ὁ τρέχων ἀνήρ, besides meaning "the running man," can also mean "the man while/when [he's] running," "the man since/because [he's] running," "the man though/although [he's] running," "the man if [he's] running," or "the man who's running." Thus, any Greek participle can potentially have a **temporal**, **causal**, **concessive**, **conditional**, or **relative** force. This requires readers of Greek to be very sensitive to context so that they may choose the *best* translation for each participle.

13.1 FINE POINTS

There's one final reason for the frequency of Greek participles: they are used in a broad variety of grammatical and syntactical environments.

1. When used with articles but without nouns (or pronouns), participles often serve as substantives:

ὁ τρέχων: the [one] running, the runner

τοὺς ἐπαινουμένους: the ones praised, the praised [ones]

2. With certain verbs, participles are often used in indirect statements (see §16.3).

3. Participles are very often used in genitive absolutes and accusative absolutes (see §14.1 and 14.2).

4. Participles serve as supplements for several very common verbs: verbs of starting, continuing, and stopping; verbs of grieving and rejoicing; τυγχάνω, φθάνω, λανθάνω.

παύομαι τρέχων: I stop running

χαίρομεν τρέχοντες: we enjoy running

ἔτυχε τρέχουσα: she happened to be running

φθάνω αὐτοὺς τρέχων: I beat them running, I'm ahead of them running

ἔλαθε τρέχων ἡμᾶς: he escaped our attention running, we didn't notice him running

5. Future participles usually convey the idea of purpose:

τρέχω βοηθήσων: I run [in order] to help

6. The particle καίπερ is always used with participles with a concessive force:

τρέχων καίπερ: although/even though running

7. Sometimes when a Contrary-to-Fact or a Future-Less-Vivid condition (see §17) is implied, but the protasis has been suppressed, the particle ἄν is used with a present or aorist participle:

εἴδομεν τὸν ἀθλητὴν ἂν ἐπαινηθέντα ὑπὸ τῶν ποιητῶν

we saw the athlete who would have been praised by the poets [if they had seen him]

σύνεσμεν τῇ ἀθλητῇ ἂν ἐπαινουμένῳ ὑπὸ τῶν ποιητῶν

we support the athlete who would be praised by the poets [if they were to see him]

As the ultimate testimony of the importance of the participle to Greek, we should note that often the most significant semantic "load" of Greek is carried not by the finite verbs of a sentence but by the participles:

He appeared, running into the shrine with many pursuers.

ἐφάνην τρέχων εἰς τὸν ἱερὸν πολλῶν διωκόντων.

Finally, when a participle expresses a fact (even an assumed fact), οὐ or one of its compounds is used to negate it; when a participle expresses some condition or contingency or even an indefinite or generic idea, it is negated by μή or one of its compounds:

οὐκ ἐπαινῶν: not praising

μή ἐπαινῶν: wouldn't be praising

ἐπαινῶν οὐδένα: praising no one

ἐπαινῶν μηδένα: praising no such person

14. ABSOLUTE CONSTRUCTIONS

Consider the following sentences:

To tell you the truth, I don't know what the answer is.

That having been said, we need to do something.

With the enemy being so near, we must guard the gates.

In each case, the underlined phrase is syntactically isolated from the main clause of the sentence, and consequently is called an **absolute** phrase. In English, such phrases can be participial or infinitival.

Such absolute phrases also occur in Greek. There are three different absolute constructions, two involving participles and one involving the infinitive.

14.1 GENITIVE ABSOLUTE

As the name suggests, in this construction a participle and its subject noun or pronoun will be in the genitive case, and that noun or pronoun is usually grammatically independent of anything in the main clause:

τῶν πολεμίων ἐγγὺς ὄντων, δεῖ ἡμᾶς φυλάττειν τὰς πύλας.

The enemy being near, we must guard the gates.

In the above sentence the absolute phrase is causal (= Since the enemy is near . . .). The relationship of the genitive absolute to the main clause can also be temporal, concessive, or conditional and is often most idiomatically translated into English with the appropriate subordinate clause rather than an absolute phrase.

Temporal:

φυγόντων τῶν πολεμίων, ἐξαίφνης ὗεν.

After the enemy fled, it suddenly rained.

[better than: With the enemy fleeing, it suddenly rained.]

Concessive:

καίπερ φυγόντων τῶν πολεμίων, δεῖ ἡμᾶς ἔτι φυλάττειν τὰς πύλας.

Although the enemy fled, we still must guard the gates.

[better than: Even with the enemy having fled, we still must guard the gates.]

Conditional:

θεῶν βουλομένων νικήσομεν τοὺς πολεμίους.

If the gods are willing, we will defeat the enemy.

[better than: With the gods willing, we will defeat the enemy.]

14.2 ACCUSATIVE ABSOLUTE

Relatively rare, this construction employs the neuter singular participle of impersonal verbs, or passive participles in the neuter singular used impersonally:

δέον φυλάττειν τὰς πύλας, πάντες ἔδραμον πρὸς τὰ τείχεα.

It being necessary to guard the gates, everyone ran toward the walls.

προσταχθὲν φυλάττειν τὰς πύλας, πάντες ἐβοηθήσαμεν.

It having been ordered to guard the gates, we all ran to help.

Personal verbs can be put into the accusative absolute construction with ὡς or ὥσπερ with the sense "in the belief that":

οἱ στρατιῶται ἔδραμον πρὸς τὰ τείχεα ὡς τοὺς πολεμίους ἐπιτιθεμένους.

The soldiers ran toward the walls, in the belief that the enemy was attacking.

14.3 INFINITIVE ABSOLUTE

Certain idiomatic phrases, particularly with verbs of speaking, constitute infinitive absolutes, commonly preceded by ὡς:

ὡς ἔπος εἰπεῖν

So to speak . . .

ὡς ἐμοὶ δοκεῖν

As it seems to me . . .

15. VERBALS

One final verb form in Greek to address is the deverbative adjective called the **verbal**. It is by no means a frequent form, but its syntax is distinctive enough to warrant mention here.

The verbal has neither a natural counterpart in English nor an easy translation. The morphology of the verbal, though, is readily identifiable: it ends in -τέος/-τέα/-τέον (usually added to the unaugmented aorist passive stem with the infix -(σ)θ- omitted). And its underlying semantic notion is also straightforward: duty, necessity, or obligation, which can often be translated with the auxiliary verb "must" or the locution "it is necessary."[1]

The verbals of intransitive verbs and transitive verbs behave differently in several important respects. The verbals of transitive verbs are usually passive and personal, and they function more like true adjectives (i.e., they emphasize the nouns they modify).

> τοῦτο ποιητέον (ἐστίν).
>
> This must be done.

> ταῦτα ποιητέα (ἐστίν).
>
> These things must be done.

> ὁ ἄγγελος πεμπτέος (ἐστίν).
>
> The messenger must be sent.

> οἱ ἄγγελοι πεμπτέοι (εἰσίν).
>
> The messengers must be sent.

Sometimes the verbal of a transitive verb can also be both active and impersonal, taking an object:

> τὴν πόλιν ὠφελητέον ἐστίν.
>
> It is necessary to benefit the city.

---

1. The Greek verbal is sometimes compared to the gerundive of Latin, which is a future passive participle used in the passive periphrastic. The comparison isn't entirely apt, however, because the verbal sometimes isn't passive and it doesn't really emphasize any futurity (in fact, it refers almost invariably to a present necessity). Just the same, the Greek verbal is used periphrastically.

δοτέον ἐστί τὰ πιστά.

It is necessary to give pledges.

The verbals of intransitive verbs are active and impersonal, and they emphasize the action of the verb (instead of modifying a noun). They are usually neuter singular, though neuter plurals can be found as well.

πειστέον ἐστίν.

It is necessary to obey.

βοηθητέον ἐστίν.

It is necessary to help.

πολεμητέα ἐστίν.

It is necessary to wage wars.

A final remark concerning verbals deals with the person(s) for whom this duty, necessity, or obligation exists. Regardless whether the construction is transitive or intransitive, personal or impersonal, verbals employ a dative of agent whenever Greek wants to say *who* must do something or *for whom* it is necessary that something be done.

τοῦτο ἐμοὶ ποιητέον (ἐστίν).

This must be done by me.

πειστέον σοὶ (ἐστίν).

It is necessary for you to obey.

τὴν πόλιν τοῖς στρατηγοῖς ὠφελητέον (ἐστίν).

It is necessary for generals to benefit the city.

16. INDIRECT STATEMENT

There are two ways to report the content of what a person says or thinks; they are referred to as **direct** and **indirect statement**. Suppose Pericles says or thinks the following sentence:

Athens is the school of Greece.

If a narrator wants to report what Pericles said or thought, he can do it through **direct statement**, reproducing the words of the original without change:

Pericles said, "Athens is the school of Greece."

Pericles thought to himself, "Athens is the school of Greece."

Or he can use the construction here defined as **indirect statement**, which entails embedding the original statement in a subordinate clause introduced by "that" (though the conjunction is often omitted in informal speech and writing):

Pericles said that Athens is/was the school of Greece.

Pericles thought that Athens is/was the school of Greece.

The choice between present and past tenses of the verb in the indirect statement is dependent on whether or not the statement is felt to have ongoing validity at the time it is being reported.

The use of indirect statement often requires changes in the exact wording of the original. A change of subject in the reported speech might be necessary:

"<u>I</u> <u>am</u> a great lover of Athens."

Pericles said that <u>he</u> <u>was</u> a great lover of Athens.

As this example also shows, a change in the tense of the verb might be required if a statement about the present or future is reported in the past and is no longer considered valid at the time of reporting (if Pericles was dead, for example). Some further examples:

"<u>I</u> <u>will lead</u> the Athenians to victory."

Pericles claimed that <u>he</u> <u>would lead</u> the Athenians to victory.

"We Athenians have assembled a great navy."

Pericles boasted that the Athenians had assembled a great navy.

Indirect statement is deployed with a great variety of verbs within the semantic sphere of speaking, thinking, feeling, or perceiving. Some of these verbs admit the substitution of an infinitive phrase in place of the subordinate clause:

I feel that this is true.

I feel this to be true.

We understand that the time has come.

We understand the time to have come.

If the subject of the infinitive is a pronoun, it will be in the objective case:

"She is a great poet."

We consider her to be a great poet.

For most verbs in this category, however, the infinitive construction is less idiomatic than the subordinate clause.

Greek also permits both the direct and indirect reporting of statements that are spoken, thought, perceived, etc.[1] To return to the example discussed above, if Pericles said,

αἱ Ἀθῆναι παίδευσις τῆς Ἑλλάδος εἰσίν.
Athens is the school of Greece.

this can be reported directly:

'αἱ Ἀθῆναι,' ἔφη ὁ Περικλῆς, 'παίδευσις τῆς Ἑλλάδος εἰσίν.'
Pericles said, "Athens is the school of Greece."

For the indirect reporting of statements, Greek offers three possible syntactic constructions for the reported statement: (1) a subordinate clause, (2) an infinitive phrase, or (3) a participial phrase. Here too it will be verbs of saying,

1. For future reference, older Greek books sometimes use Latin to refer to direct statement as ***oratio recta*** and indirect statement as ***oratio obliqua***.

thinking, perceiving, or feeling that require one of these constructions. The choice of construction in a particular situation is partly dependent on the main verb, although several verbs offer the choice of more than one construction.

16.1 SUBORDINATE CLAUSE

The subordinating conjunction corresponding to English "that" is either ὅτι or ὡς, and it cannot be omitted. This construction is found with the verb λέγω, and certain verbs of knowing and perception. If the main verb is in a primary tense, the verb in the indirect statement retains its tense and mood, although the subject may change, as may any personal pronouns:

'βασιλεὺς τῶν Περσῶν εἰμι.'
"I am the king of the Persians."

ὁ Ξέρξης λέγει ὅτι βασιλεὺς τῶν Περσῶν ἐστιν.
Xerxes says that he is the king of the Persians.

τρεῖς δοῦλοι ἔφυγον.
Three slaves escaped.

οὐκ οἶσθα ὡς τρεῖς δοῦλοι ἔφυγον;
Do you not know that three slaves escaped?

If the main verb is in a secondary tense, the verb in the indirect statement may remain unchanged or it may be changed to the optative of the same tense:

ὁ Ξέρξης εἶπεν ὅτι βασιλεὺς τῶν Περσῶν εἴη (or ἐστιν).
Xerxes said that he was the king of the Persians.

ἆρα ἤκουσας ὡς τρεῖς δοῦλοι φύγοιεν (or ἔφυγον);
Did you hear that three slaves escaped?

Note in the first example that Greek retains the present tense of the indirect statement when the main verb is in the past, even if the statement is no longer valid.

16.2 INFINITIVE PHRASE

Certain verbs govern an infinitive phrase of indirect statement, including verbs of saying (sometimes λέγω and almost always φημί), and especially verbs of thinking (νομίζω, οἴομαι, etc.). In this construction the finite verb of the direct statement is changed into the same tense of the infinitive (imperfect forms become present infinitives, pluperfects become perfect infinitives). If the subject of the infinitive is the same as that of the main verb, it is left unexpressed; if it is different, it is put in the accusative case. A negative (οὐ or μή) in the original statement generally remains unchanged.

βαίνω πρὸς τὸν θέατρον.
I am going to the theater.

φημὶ βαίνειν πρὸς τὸν θέατρον.
I say that I am going to the theater.

οὐδείς με φιλεῖ.
Nobody loves me.

ἐνόμιζεν οὐδένα φιλεῖν αὐτόν.
He thought that nobody loved him.

τιμήσουσιν οἱ πολῖται τὸν νικῶντα.
The citizens will honor the victor.

ἔφην τοὺς πολίτας τιμήσειν τὸν νικῶντα.
I said that the citizens would honor the victor.

If the direct statement contains an indicative or optative with the particle ἄν, the particle is retained with the infinitive:

ῥᾳδίως ἂν κρατήσαιμεν τοὺς πολεμίους.
We would easily defeat the enemy.

οἴομαι ἡμᾶς ῥᾳδίως ἂν κρατῆσαι τοὺς πολεμίους.
I believe that we would easily defeat the enemy.

16.3 PARTICIPIAL PHRASE

Finally, many verbs introducing indirect statement can take a supplementary participle, especially verbs of perception (ἀκούω, πυνθάνομαι, etc.), verbal demonstration (δείκνυμι, ἀγγέλλω, etc.), or seeming (φαίνομαι). Here too, the participle will be in the same tense as the verb of the direct statement and will take the same case as its subject. If the subject of the indirect statement is different from that of the main verb, it will be in the accusative case:

ὁ κλὼψ ἐκ τοῦ δεσμοτηρίου ἔφυγεν.
The thief escaped from the prison.

ἐπυθόμεθα τὸν κλῶπα ἐκ τοῦ δεσμοτηρίου φυγόντα.
We learned that the thief had escaped from the prison.

οὗτος ὁ ἀνὴρ κακοποιός ἐστιν.
This man is an evildoer.

δείξω τοῦτον τὸν ἄνδρα κακοποιὸν ὄντα.
I will show that this man is an evildoer.

If the subjects of the main verb and participle are the same, the subject of the participle is left unexpressed and the participle is in the nominative case:

ὁ Σωκράτης σοφώτατός ἐστιν.
Socrates is the wisest man.

ὁ Σωκράτης φαίνεται σοφώτατος ὤν.
Socrates seems to be the wisest man.

As was true of the infinitive construction, if the direct statement contains an indicative or optative with the particle ἄν, the particle is retained with the participle:

ῥᾳδίως ἂν κρατήσαιμεν τοὺς πολεμίους.
We would easily defeat the enemy.

ἔδειξε ἡμᾶς ῥᾳδίως ἂν κρατήσαντας τοὺς πολεμίους.
He pointed out that we would easily defeat the enemy.

16.4 DEPENDENT CLAUSES

In many languages, the syntax of dependent clauses within indirect statement is quite complicated, but the rules in Greek are relatively few and straightforward. The rules in modern English, though not numerous, are mostly ignored in everyday speech.

The first thing to understand is the structure of these complex sentences. They consist of at least three major parts: the main clause, the principal clause within the subordinate clause, and the dependent clause within the subordinate clause.

We understand	that they will show up tomorrow, unless it rains in the morning.
MAIN CLAUSE	SUBORDINATE CLAUSE

they will show up	unless it rains in the morning.
PRINCIPAL CLAUSE	DEPENDENT CLAUSE

In both Greek and English, the syntax of the principal clause is determined by the construction of the indirect statement. That is, for Greek, if the verb of the main clause requires an infinitive or a participle, the verb of the principal clause will be an infinitive or participle; if the verb of the main clause requires the use of ὡς or ὅτι and a finite verb, the verb of the principal clause will be finite after ὡς or ὅτι. So a good grasp of the rules of indirect statement addresses half of the syntax, provided that you identify correctly which of the subordinate clauses is the principal one.

On the whole, the syntax of the dependent clause is determined by the type of clause found there. For example, if the dependent clause is conditional, it follows the rules for conditionals (see §17); if the dependent clause is temporal, it follows the rules for temporal clauses (see §24); if the dependent clause is a result clause, it follows the rules for result clauses (see §21); or if the dependent clause is an infinitive or participial phrase, it follows the rules for infinitive and participial phrases (see §§12 and 13).

You get the idea now. Principal clauses behave according to indirect statement. Dependent clauses behave according to their subordinate-clause type. Easy!

Well, sort of. With Greek verbs, we always need to consider mood as well as tense. With three moods at play (indicative, subjunctive, and optative) and two sequences of tenses (primary and secondary), we'll examine six permutations.

(A) If the verb in the main clause is primary (that is, present, future, perfect, or future perfect), the verb of the dependent clause will retain the same tense and mood as if the sentence had been one of direct statement.

He understands that Xerxes is coming in order to defeat Greece.

γιγνώσκει ὅτι ὁ Ξέρξης ἐπέρχεται ἵνα νικᾷ [present subjunctive] τὴν Ἑλλάδα.

He understands that Xerxes came in order to defeat Greece.

γιγνώσκει ὅτι ὁ Ξέρξης ἐπῆλθεν ἵνα νικῴη [present optative] (or νικᾷ [present subjunctive]) τὴν Ἑλλάδα.

But if the verb of the main clause is secondary (that is, imperfect, aorist, or pluperfect), several options emerge. (B) If the dependent verb would be in a primary tense of the indicative or subjunctive had the sentence been one of direct statement, in indirect statement it can retain the same tense and mood, *or* it can go into the optative mood (without ἄν).[2]

He understood that Xerxes has come in order to defeat Greece.

ἔγνω ὅτι ὁ Ξέρξης ἐπιληλυθὼς εἴη (or ἐπελήλυθε) ἵνα νικᾷ [present subjunctive] (or νικῴη [present optative]) τὴν Ἑλλάδα.

(C) If the dependent verb is in a primary tense of the optative (with or without ἄν), it will remain in the optative mood (with or without ἄν).

He understood that that Xerxes came since he might be greedy.

ἔγνω ὅτι ὁ Ξέρξης ἐπέλθοι (or ἐπῆλθε) ἐπειδὰν εἴη [present optative] πλεονεκτικός.

(D) But if the dependent verb would be in a secondary tense of the indicative if the sentence had been one of direct statement, it will usually remain in the indicative mood in an indirect statement.[3]

2. Note how these compounds of ἄν behave: If, in direct statement, ἐάν is used with a subjunctive, in the dependent clause of an indirect statement it will be converted to εἰ if the dependent verb is optative. In similar circumstances, ὅταν, ὁπόταν, ἐπάν (or ἐπήν), and ἐπειδάν are converted to ὅτε, ὁπότε, ἐπεί, and ἐπειδή.

3. While an imperfect indicative in an indirect statement may rarely be found converted to a present optative or a pluperfect indicative converted to a perfect optative, an aorist indicative (unlike an aorist subjunctive) is never converted in an indirect statement to an aorist optative. This fact further attests to the special nature of the aorist tense (see §11.4).

He understood that that Xerxes came to Greece, where the unrest had begun.

ἔγνω ὅτι ὁ Ξέρξης ἐπέλθοι (or ἐπῆλθε) ἐπὶ τὴν Ἑλλάδα οὗ ἡ στάσις ἐγεγόνει [pluperfect indicative].

(E) If the dependent verb would be in a secondary tense of the subjunctive if the sentence had been one of direct statement, in an indirect statement the dependent verb can remain in the subjunctive mood *or* it can go into the optative mood (without ἄν).

He understood that that Xerxes came in order to defeat Greece.

ἔγνω ὅτι ὁ Ξέρξης ἐπέλθοι (or ἐπῆλθε) ἵνα νικήσῃ [aorist subjunctive] (or νικήσειε [aorist optative]) τὴν Ἑλλάδα.

(F) Finally, if the dependent verb would be in a secondary tense of the optative (with or without ἄν) if the sentence had been one of direct statement, in an indirect statement it will remain in the optative mood (with or without ἄν).

He understood that that Xerxes came since he might defeat Greece.

ἔγνω ὅτι ὁ Ξέρξης ἐπέλθοι (or ἐπῆλθε) ἐπειδὰν νικήσειε [aorist optative] τὴν Ἑλλάδα.

Let's consider the matter in tabular form; the following illustrates the moods of dependent clauses in indirect statement:

CLAUSE:	MAIN		PRINCIPAL		DEPENDENT	
	Tense	Mood	Tense	Mood	Tense	Mood
(A)	1°	*	**	**	1° or 2°	Indicative, Subjunctive, or Optative
(B)	2°	*	**	**	1°	Indicative, Subjunctive, or Optative.***
(C)	2°	*	**	**	1°	Optative
(D)	2°	*	**	**	2°	Indicative
(E)	2°	*	**	**	2°	Subjunctive or Optative ***
(F)	2°	*	**	**	2°	Optative

NOTES:

1° = primary tense; 2° = secondary tense

* Any of the moods; irrelevant for illustration.

** Tense and/or mood are determined by the syntax of the main clause.

*** With no particular semantic difference.

For purposes of comparison, the following table illustrates how the subordinate clauses of the same sentences would be expressed in direct statement:

CLAUSE:	MAIN		SUBORDINATE	
	Tense	Mood	Tense	Mood
(A)	1°	*	1° or 2 °	Indicative, Subjunctive, or Optative **
(B)	2°	*	1°	Indicative or Subjunctive **
(C)	2°	*	1°	Optative **
(D)	2°	*	2°	Indicative **
(E)	2°	*	2°	Subjunctive **
(F)	2°	*	2°	Optative **

NOTES:

1° = primary tense; 2° = secondary tense

* Any of the moods; irrelevant for illustration.

** Tense and/or mood are determined by the syntax of the main clause.

17. CONDITIONALS

Many linguists and logicians claim that **conditional sentences** are the most difficult business any language has to do. This claim is explained by the fact that conditional sentences reflect contingent thinking and their expression requires a clear distinction between real, potential, and unreal contingencies. Not all practitioners of language fully apprehend the linguistic and/or logical distinctions of these contingencies. Hence the fundamental difficulty.

This difficulty can be avoided if the language student grasps the inherent clarity and structure of conditional sentences. In other words, that area of "language logic" often cited as the most difficult is, in fact, easily comprehensible with the proper analytical tools.

Conditional sentences can be distinguished in terms of their relationship to time, in terms of their relationship to reality, and in terms of their structures and components.

To be more specific, conditional sentences express contingencies that existed (or didn't exist) in the past, that exist (or don't exist) in the present, or that will exist (or may exist) in the future. Likewise, some contingencies are very likely to be fulfilled, others cannot be fulfilled, while still others may or may not be fulfilled.

As to structure, conditionals are typically complex sentences, consisting of a main clause (often called the **apodosis**) and a subordinate clause (often called the **protasis**).

If Alexander attacks, our hopes are over.

[PROTASIS] [APODOSIS]

The protasis is sometimes referred to as the "if-clause," the "assumption," or the "proposition," while the apodosis can be referred to as the "then-clause," the "conclusion," or the "consequence."[1]

1. Etymologically, the Latinate "proposition" and Greek "protasis" mean about the same thing: "a thing set forth." The Greek apodosis means "a payoff."

It's worth noting at this juncture that the if-clause (protasis) in English and in Greek doesn't always precede the then-clause (apodosis). In fact, from a rhetorical standpoint, sometimes an apodosis placed prior to its protasis imparts a greater punchiness. Consider:

> You *will* succeed in life, if you study Greek.
>
> If you study Greek, you will succeed in life.

Basically, we distinguish the protasis from the apodosis in English by means of the conditional subordinating conjunction used in the protasis: "if," "unless," etc. Likewise, Greek will always use a subordinating conjunction in the protasis, but in certain contexts it will also use a coordinating conjunction in the apodosis. Because conditional sentences rely on clauses, and because clauses rely on verbs, and because verbs rely on the notion of tense and aspect, you will find that the principles of tense and aspect (see §11.4) are completely at play in Greek conditionals. That is, theoretically, all of the Greek tenses can be found in conditionals, and the aspectual distinctions of aoristic and imperfective are also fully operative in conditionals. Thus, Greek conditionals can be broadly thought of as operating in the past, present, and future, and as occurring as either one-time actions or repeated actions.

Conditionals can also be classified as real, potential, or unreal. This distinction speaks to their **vividness**, that is, the likelihood of their fulfillment. Unreal conditions cannot be fulfilled; a potential condition may or may not be fulfilled; and a real or factual condition will or won't be fulfilled. In Greek, the distinctions of vividness are made, at least in part, by means of the moods (see §11.7) of the verbs employed in the conditional sentences; in English, the distinctions are made by means of moods and the auxiliary verbs employed.

> If it <u>were</u> rain<u>ing</u> today [but it isn't], they <u>would</u>n't play the game.: UNREAL
>
> Maybe, if it <u>were to/should</u> rain today, we <u>would</u>n't need to water the lawn.: POTENTIAL
>
> Even if it [actually] rains today, the no-burn order is still in effect.: REAL or FACTUAL

17.1 SIMPLE

The most vivid conditions are called **simple conditionals** or **particular conditionals** because they express a fairly direct and automatic vividness between the protasis and apodosis:

> If you stick your finger in this light socket, you get a shock.

The directness, or "is-ness," of this relationship naturally relies on the indicative mood, which is, as we saw in §11.7.1, the mood of factual assertion.

In Greek, the if-word with the indicative is εἰ.

17.2 GENERAL

General conditionals, inasmuch as they are not simple or specific but generalize, move away from the indicative realm of "is-ness" into the more general and vague realm of "maybe-ness":

> If ever you stick your finger in a light socket [which you may or may not do], you get a shock.

As we saw in §11.7.3 and §11.7.4, the subjunctive and optative moods most properly accommodate notions of "maybe-ness."

In Greek, the if-word with the subjunctive is ἐάν, and with the optative is εἰ.

17.3 FUTURE

Future conditionals express conditions which will (or will not) be fulfilled in the future. Differences of vividness in English are expressed by the presence, absence, and choice of modal auxiliaries.:

> More Vivid: If you stick your finger in the light socket, you will get a shock.

The protasis here expresses an obvious contingency (that is, you may or may not stick your finger in the socket), so the subjunctive mood (as a mood of contingency) makes sense. The apodosis expresses a future reality, so the future indicative makes sense.

Again, in Greek, the if-word with the subjunctive is ἐάν.

> Less Vivid: If you were to/should stick your finger in the light socket, you would get a shock.

Here, the protasis sounds less likely to be fulfilled (i.e., more contingent), thus justifying an optative verb in Greek. And since the protasis is less likely, the apodosis is similarly remote, and it too justifies an optative.

Again, in Greek, the if-word with the optative is εἰ. The greater remoteness in the apodosis is expressed by the addition of the particle ἄν.

17.4 CONTRARY TO FACT

Finally, some conditions are clearly **contrary to fact** (or **contrafactual**) and **unreal**; that is, they have absolutely no likelihood of being fulfilled. One could say that their very unreality is factual, and insofar as the indicative is the mood of the factual, it's therefore reasonable to find the indicative (imperfect for present contrafactuals, aorist for past contrafactuals) used with unreal conditions:[2]

> If you had stuck your knee in this light socket [but you didn't], you would have gotten a shock.

Again, the Greek if-word with the indicative is εἰ. The complete remoteness of the apodosis in contrafactuals calls for the addition of the particle ἄν.

17.5 MIXED

Mixed conditionals are sentences which use one type of condition in the protasis and another type in the apodosis. Not especially common, they are easy

2. This apparent paradox is underscored (or perhaps softened) by the required use of the particle ἄν in the apodosis of contrafactuals, as if to signal that the indicative is serving to positively affirm an unreal condition.

enough to identify because each clause conforms to the syntax of its distinct type; e.g.,

> If Alexander had already come, he would now be defeating them.
>
> εἰ ὁ Ἀλέξανδρος ἔβη, ἂν αὐτοὺς ἐνίκα.

Here the protasis is a past contrafactual (notice the aorist indicative), while the apodosis is a present contrafactual (notice the imperfect indicative with ἄν). Or, again,

> If Alexander ever comes, he will defeat them.
>
> ἐὰν ὁ Ἀλέξανδρος βαίνῃ, αὐτοὺς νικήσει.

In this conditional, we find a present general condition in the protasis (notice the subjunctive with ἐάν) and a future most vivid in the apodosis (notice the future indicative).

Similarly, conditions can be found in sentences of mixed syntax. For example,

> If Alexander is coming, defeat him!
>
> εἰ ὁ Ἀλέξανδρος βαίνει, νικήσατε αὐτόν.

Here we have a present simple condition in the protasis, but the apodosis consists of an imperative. Or, again,

> If Alexander should come, what are we to do?
>
> εἰ ὁ Ἀλέξανδρος βαίνοι, τί πράττωμεν;

The protasis in this case marks it as a Future-Less-Vivid condition, but the apodosis presents a deliberative subjunctive (see §11.7.3).

Sometimes, the protasis of a conditional sentence can be expressed by means of a participle, especially in a genitive absolute:

> If Alexander is coming, we will retreat.
>
> Ἀλεξάνδρου βαίνοντος, ἀποχωρήσομεν.

See §§13 and 14 for further discussion on this construction.

The conjunctions and particles used with Greek conditional sentences are particularly useful in identifying the types of conditions. For example, ἐάν is only used in the protasis with a verb in the subjunctive mood in either a Present General or a Future-More-Vivid condition, depending on the structure of the apodosis. Likewise, ἄν in the apodosis signals either a Contrary-to-Fact condition if used with an indicative or a Future-Less-Vivid condition if used with an optative.

Finally, note that Greek uses different adverbs for negating the protasis (μή and its compounds) and negating the apodosis (οὐ/οὐκ/οὐχ and its compounds).

In sum, if you master the inflectional forms distinguishing tense, aspect, and mood, as well as the few conditional conjunctions and particles, you will experience no difficulty whatsoever with Greek conditional sentences.

As you review the following conditional sentences, which exemplify all the different types, pay careful attention to the moods, tenses, aspects, particles, and conjunctions in action:

I. Simple or Particular

A. Present

εἰ τοῦτο ποιεῖς, σὲ παύω.

If you do this, I stop you.

B. Past

εἰ τοῦτο ἐποίεις, σὲ ἔπαυον.

If you were doing this, I was stopping you.

εἰ τοῦτο ἐποίησας, σὲ ἔπαυσα.

If you did this, I stopped you.

II. General

A. Present

ἐὰν τοῦτο ποιῇς, σὲ παύω.

If you ever [repeatedly] do this, I [always] stop you.

ἐὰν τοῦτο ποιήσῃς, σὲ παύω.

If you ever [once] do this, I [always] stop you.

B. Past

εἰ τοῦτο ποιοῖς, σὲ ἔπαυον.

If you ever [repeatedly] did this, I [always] stopped you.

εἰ τοῦτο ποιήσαις, σὲ ἔπαυον.

If you ever [once] did this, I [always] stopped you.

III. Contrary-to-Fact or Contrafactual or Unreal

A. Present

εἰ τοῦτο ἐποίεις, σὲ ἂν ἔπαυον.

If you were [right now] doing this [but you aren't], I would stop you.

B. Past

εἰ τοῦτο ἐποίησας, σὲ ἂν ἔπαυσα.

If you had done this [but you didn't], I would have stopped you.

IV. Future

A. More Vivid

ἐὰν τοῦτο ποιῇς, σὲ παύσω.

If you do this [repeatedly], I will stop you.

ἐὰν τοῦτο ποιήσῃς, σὲ παύσω.

If you do this [once], I will stop you.

B. Less Vivid

εἰ τοῦτο ποιοῖς, σὲ ἂν παύοιμι.

If you should do this [repeatedly], I would stop you [repeatedly].

If you were to do this [repeatedly], I would stop you [repeatedly].

εἰ τοῦτο ποιήσαις, σὲ ἂν παύσαιμι.

If you should do this [once], I would stop you [once].

If you were to do this [once], I would stop you [once].

C. Most Vivid[3]

εἰ τοῦτο ποιήσεις, σὲ παύσω.

If you will do this [either repeatedly or once], I will stop you.

3. Some grammar books treat this as a simple condition.

V. Mixed: e.g.,

ἐὰν τοῦτο ποιήσῃς, σὲ ἂν παύσαιμι.

If you do this [once], I would stop you.

PROTASIS: Future More Vivid; APODOSIS: Future Less Vivid

εἰ τοῦτο ἐποίησας, σὲ παύω.

If you did this thing [before], I stop you [now].

PROTASIS: Past Simple; APODOSIS: Present Simple

ἐὰν τοῦτο ποιήσῃς, σὲ παύσω.

If you ever [once] do this, I will stop you.

PROTASIS: Present General; APODOSIS: Future More/Most Vivid

The following represents a tabular summary of the syntactical information about Greek conditionals:

TIME	TYPE	PROTASIS	APODOSIS
PRESENT	Simple	εἰ with present or perfect indicative	present or perfect indicative
	Contrafactual	εἰ with imperfect indicative	imperfect indicative with ἄν
	General	ἐάν with a subjunctive	present indicative
PAST	Simple	εἰ with imperfect, aorist, or pluperfect indicative	imperfect, aorist, or pluperfect indicative
	Contrafactual	εἰ with aorist indicative	aorist indicative with ἄν
	General	εἰ with an optative	imperfect indicative
FUTURE	More Vivid	ἐάν with a subjunctive	future indicative
	Less Vivid	εἰ with an optative	optative with ἄν
	Most Vivid	εἰ with future indicative	future indicative
	Mixed	[any of the above, true to its particular type]	[any of the above, true to its particular type]

18. CONCESSIVE CLAUSES

We should mention an important subcategory of conditionals called **concessive clauses**. In English, concessive clauses are commonly introduced by the conjunctions "although," "though," "even though," and "even if"; a coordinating sentence adverb like "however," "nonetheless," "nevertheless," or "even so" can often be found in the main clause, particularly when the concessive clause precedes the main clause.

Concessive clauses can be understood as the protasis of a conditional sentence where the apodosis will be fulfilled regardless of whether or not the protasis is true.

Even if/although Pericles is ill, we will leave.

In the sentence above the speakers will leave irrespective of Pericles' current health status. Contrast the conditional:

If Pericles is ill, we will leave.

In this sentence, the truth of the speakers' departure is conditioned entirely on Pericles' ill health. Presumably, if Pericles is not ill, the speakers will stay.

In Greek, the conditional nature of concessive clauses is revealed by the conjunctions used: εἰ καί or καί εἰ (crasis: κεἰ), ἐὰν καί or καὶ ἐάν (crasis: κἄν). εἰ καί and καί εἰ introduce concessive clauses that are simple/particular, contrafactual, past general, future most vivid, and future less vivid; ἐὰν καί and καὶ ἐάν introduce concessive clauses that are present general and future more vivid. In other words, εἰ and ἐάν are found in concessive clauses exactly as we learned them for the protasis of conditional clauses. Where concessive clauses are used, however, the main clauses do not necessarily behave like the apodosis of conditional sentences.

εἰ καὶ/καὶ εἰ/κεἰ τοῦτο ποιεῖς, ἐσμέν εὐδαίμονες.

Although you do this, we are happy. [SIMPLE PRESENT]

εἰ καὶ/καὶ εἰ/κεἰ τοῦτο ἐποίησας, ἐσμέν εὐδαίμονες.

Although you did this, we are happy. [SIMPLE PAST]

Even if you had done this [but you didn't], we are happy. [CONTRAFACTUAL]

εἰ καὶ/καὶ εἰ/κεἰ τοῦτο ποιήσαις, ἐσμέν εὐδαίμονες.
Even if you ever did this, we are happy. [GENERAL PAST]

εἰ καὶ/καὶ εἰ/κεἰ τοῦτο ποιοῖς, ἐσμέν εὐδαίμονες.
Even though you were to do this, we are happy. [LESS VIVID]

ἐὰν καὶ/καὶ ἐὰν/κἂν τοῦτο ποιῇς, ἐσμέν εὐδαίμονες.
Even if you ever do this, we are happy. [GENERAL PRESENT]

ἐὰν καὶ/καὶ ἐὰν/κἂν τοῦτο ποιήσῃς, ἐσμέν εὐδαίμονες.
Although you do this [in the future], we are happy. [MORE VIVID]

Concessive clauses are negated by μή (or one of its compounds).

An alternate (and simpler) way of expressing concessive clauses is with participles (whether in absolutes or not), often with the particle καίπερ. See §13.

19. RELATIVE CLAUSES

A **relative clause** is a subordinate clause that is introduced by a relative pronoun (see §§8.4, 9.2) or a relative adverb (see below). The English relative pronouns are "who," "whom," "whose," "which," "what," "that," "who(so)ever," "whom(so)ever," "which(so)ever," and "what(so)ever." Some of these, like the personal pronouns, are marked for case (subjective, objective, possessive) and gender (masculine/feminine, neuter):

who: subjective, masculine/feminine, singular and plural

whom: objective, masculine/feminine, singular and plural

whose: possessive, masculine/feminine and neuter, singular and plural

which: subjective and objective, neuter, singular and plural

The pronoun "that" can be singular or plural, masculine/feminine or neuter, subjective or objective. "What" stands in for "that which," and is always neuter:

I don't agree with what you say. = I don't agree with that (thing) which you say.

Syntactically, relative clauses can function as either adjectival phrases or noun phrases. In the former case, the noun which the clause modifies is called its **antecedent**. In theory, the relative pronoun must agree with this antecedent in number and gender, but owing to its very limited declension, in practice this is an issue in only a few instances:

Themistocles devised a strategy which (not who) led to victory. [NEUTER]

We need a leader who (not which) can inspire the people. [MASCULINE/FEMININE]

The substitution of "that" for "who" or "which" eliminates even this gender distinction:

Themistocles devised a strategy that led to victory.

We need a leader that can inspire the people.

Although the relative pronouns do not show a morphological distinction between singular and plural, their number may become relevant if they serve as the subject of the verb in their clause:

I don't trust a person who always agrees with me. ["who" is singular]

I don't trust people who always agree with me. ["who" is plural]

If the relative pronoun serves some other function in its clause besides the subject, it is this function that determines its case:

The man who loves the city wins great praise. ["who" is the subject of "loves"]

The man whom the city loves wins great praise. ["whom" is the object of "loves"]

The man whose city is rich is never poor. ["whose" is a possessive, with city]

Relative pronouns in the objective case are sometimes omitted in less formal writing or speech, if this can be done without awkwardness or ambiguity:

The man the city loves wins great praise.

There are two ways in which an adjectival relative clause can modify its antecedent. A so-called **nonrestrictive** clause simply adds further information about the antecedent, and its deletion would not affect the validity of the sentence:

Thucydides, who was an Athenian general, wrote a history of the war with Sparta.

A **restrictive** clause, on the other hand, places a limit on the range of its antecedent, and its deletion would often result in an overly broad statement that thereby becomes invalid. In the English system of punctuation, it is generally not set off by commas:

Athenian generals who were also historians were very rare.

When the antecedent of the relative pronoun is indefinite ("he who," "anyone who"), it can be omitted, though the result is often not very idiomatic:

He who laughs last, laughs best. → Who laughs last, laughs best.

More idiomatic is to replace the simple relative with the indefinite forms "whoever," "whomever," "whichever." The resulting clause functions as a noun rather than an adjective:

> Whoever says this is lying. ["Whoever says this" is the subject of "is"]
>
> I trust whomever you trust. ["whomever you trust" is the object of "trust"]

The pronouns "which" and "what" can sometimes refer to an entire clause as their antecedent:

> He announced that the army had been victorious, which made everyone rejoice.

Finally, clauses headed by relative adverbs function adverbially:

> When(ever) it rains, it pours.
>
> Where(ever) there is smoke, there is fire.
>
> How(ever) you answer this will decide your fate.

The indefinite adverbs are noted here with the suffix *-ever* added parenthetically.

The basic grammatical principles governing the Greek relative clause are essentially the same as the English. The difference is that such clauses are far more frequent in Greek, and they show a far greater range of syntactic uses.

Because the Greek relative pronoun is fully inflected, the rules governing agreement and case are transparent: the pronoun will regularly take the gender and number of its antecedent, and its case will be determined by its grammatical function within its clause.

> ὁ στρατηγὸς ὃς τοὺς Πέρσας ἐνίκησεν μάλιστα ἐτιμήθη.
>
> The general, who defeated the Persians, was very greatly honored.
>
> ὁ στρατηγὸς ὃν οἱ Πέρσαι ἐνίκησαν μάλιστα ἐμέμφθη.
>
> The general, whom the Persians defeated, was very greatly reviled.
>
> αἱ γυναῖκες ὧν ἄνδρες μάχονται πολλὰ πάσχουσιν.
>
> The women whose husbands are fighting suffer much.

αἱ γυναῖκες αἷς ὁ ἄγγελος τὴν νίκην ἤγγειλεν ἔχαιρον.

The women, to whom the messenger announced the victory, rejoiced.

Like all adverbs, relative adverbs are indeclinable:

οὗ οἱ πολῖται τοὺς θεοὺς οὐ φοβοῦνται, ἀσθενεῖ ἡ δίκη.

Where the citizens do not fear the gods, justice withers.

The relative can serve to link two sentences together, in which case it is often better translated with a personal pronoun:

τίς ἂν πιστεύοι ἐκείνῳ τῷ ῥήτορι; ὃς πολλάκις ψεύδει τὸν δῆμον.

Who would trust that speaker? He often deceives the people.

Corresponding to the English "which" or "what," the neuter relative pronoun can have an entire clause as its antecedent, although in Greek the relative clause often comes first:

ὃ ἡμῖν γελοιότατον ἐδόκει, ὁ ἵππος ἤρξατο ὄρχεσθαι.

What seemed most ridiculous to us, the horse began to dance.

The rule governing the case of the relative pronoun is occasionally violated by the phenomenon of **attraction**, where the pronoun is "attracted" into the case of its antecedent, particularly when the pronoun would otherwise be in the accusative case and the antecedent is either dative or genitive:

ἔρχομαι μετὰ τοῦ ἀδελφοῦ, οὗ γιγνώσκεις. (οὗ rather than ὃν)

I am coming with my brother, whom you know.

On occasion you may also encounter an example of reverse attraction, where the antecedent is attracted to the case of the relative pronoun, as determined by its function in its clause. To link the antecedent and relative pronoun even more closely, the antecedent may be incorporated into the relative clause itself and take on the case of the pronoun:

ποῦ εὑρήσομεν ὃς ἡμᾶς σώσει ἀνήρ;

Where will we find a man who will save us?

rather than

ποῦ εὑρήσομεν ἄνδρα ὃς ἡμᾶς σώσει;

19.1 FINE POINTS:

Far beyond their potential in English, Greek relative clauses can encompass many other syntactic functions. In many cases it is not possible to retain the relative structure in an idiomatic English translation.

(1) Imperative: πέμψω σοι ἐπιστολὴν ἣν ἀκριβῶς ἀναγίγνωσκε.
I will send you a letter. Read it carefully.

(2) Wish: μισῶ τοὺς ῥήτορας οὓς οἱ θεοὶ ἀπωλέσειαν.
I hate the politicians. May the gods destroy them!

(3) Relative clauses of purpose generally take the future indicative in Attic Greek: οἱ Ἀθηναῖοι ἔπεμψαν ἀγγέλους οἳ σπείσονται εἰρήνην.
The Athenians sent messengers who were to conclude a peace treaty.

(4) Relative clauses of result generally take the indicative as well: τίς οὕτω μωρός ἐστι ὅστις οὐ φοβεῖται τὰ δῶρα τὰ τῶν Ἑλλήνων.
Who is so foolish that he does not fear Greek gifts?

(5) Conditions: Relative clauses can function as the protasis of any type of condition; the mood and tense of its verb will follow the general rules governing conditional sentences of that particular type (for which see §17). For example, in a relative clause functioning as the protasis of a general condition, its verb will be subjunctive or optative, depending on the tense of the main verb: ὅστις ἂν τοῦτο ἴδῃ, θαυμάζει. (= εἴ τις ἂν τοῦτο ἴδῃ . . .)
Whoever sees this is amazed.

ὅστις τοῦτο ἴδοι, ἐθαύμασεν. (= εἴ τις τοῦτο ἴδοι . . .)
Whoever saw this was amazed.

20. PURPOSE CLAUSES

Purpose clauses (also known as **final clauses**) answer the question, "to what end?" or "for what effect?" the action of the main verb is performed. In English, the minimal structure of a purpose clause looks like this:

He rose to greet me.[1]

But this is only a shortened form of the more expansive:

He rose in order to greet me. *or*

He rose so to greet me.[2]

And for these there are two conjunctive alternatives:

He rose in order that he might greet me.

He rose so that he might greet me.

When the subject of the subordinate clause differs from the subject of the main verb, English offers these options:

He sent them to greet me.

He sent them in order to greet me.

He sent them in order that they might greet me.

He sent them so that they might greet me.

He sent them that they might greet me.

In formal English, when the main verb is in the present, future, or present perfect tense, the auxiliary verb *may* is required in the purpose clause; when the main verb is in any of the other past tenses, the auxiliary verb *might* is required in the purpose clause:

She sends us in order that we may greet them.

She has sent us so that we may greet them.

---

1. Be careful not to confuse purpose clauses with complementary infinitives (e.g., "he desires to greet me") which typically express need, effort, or intention.

2. Consider the archaic and poetic: He rose for to greet me.

She was sending us in order that we <u>might</u> greet them.

She had sent us so that we <u>might</u> greet them.

In the English of common, everyday usage, however, these auxiliaries are usually omitted.

Greek also has several alternatives for expressing the notion of purpose. We've seen future participles used to this end (see §13); and even genitive articular infinitives (see §12) with the preposition ὑπέρ or the postposition ἕνεκα. In the preceding chapter (§19), we learned that relative clauses with the future indicative can express purpose, too. Consider:

They listen in order to understand.

γνωσόμενοι ἀκούουσιν.

ὑπὲρ τοῦ γιγνώσκειν ἀκούουσιν.

τοῦ γιγνώσκειν ἕνεκα ἀκούουσιν.

οἳ γνώσονται ἀκούουσιν.

The more common construction, though, involves a subordinate clause introduced by one of the Greek final conjunctions: ἵνα, ὅπως, or ὡς. Purpose clauses are negated either by the addition of μή to these conjunctions or by their replacement with μή.[3]

The syntax of Greek purpose clauses is fairly straightforward: if the main verb is in a primary tense (i.e., present, future, perfect, or future perfect), the subordinate verb is in the subjunctive mood; but if the main verb is in a secondary tense (i.e., imperfect, aorist, or pluperfect), the subordinate verb can be in the subjunctive mood or, more commonly, the optative mood.

ἀκούομεν ἵνα/ὅπως/ὡς γιγνώσκωμεν.

We listen in order to understand.

ἠκούομεν ἵνα/ὅπως/ὡς γιγνώσκοιμεν (or γιγνώσκωμεν).

We were listening so that we might understand.

3. Now obsolescent, the English conjunction "lest" means "so that not" or "in order that not." It can often be found in older translations, but it is extremely rare in modern American speech except in frozen phrases like "lest we forget."

οὐκ ἀκούομεν (ἵνα/ὅπως/ὡς) μὴ γιγνώσκωμεν.

We don't listen so that we may not understand.

οὐκ ἠκούομεν (ἵνα/ὅπως/ὡς) μὴ γιγνώσκοιμεν (or γιγνώσκωμεν).

We weren't listening in order that we might not understand.

21. RESULT CLAUSES

Result clauses (also known as **consecutive clauses**) are subordinate clauses which answer the question, "to what extent?" or "to what degree?" was the action or condition of the main verb carried to an outcome.

He is so unhappy <u>that he doesn't eat</u>.

She became such a good speaker <u>that everyone respected her</u>.

We caught so many fish <u>that we reached the limit within an hour</u>.

They acted in such a way <u>as to confuse us</u>.

I will complain so much to the owner <u>as to get my money back</u>.

With these examples, you'll notice that the first three sentences represent real or actual results, while the latter two sentences represent expected or potential results. You'll also notice that the result clauses are triggered by the adverbs "so" and "such," which help distinguish result clauses from purpose clauses (see §20):

They acted this way (so) to confuse us. [PURPOSE]

They acted in such a way as to confuse us. [RESULT]

She became a good speaker in order that everyone might respect her. [PURPOSE]

She became such a good speaker that everyone respected her. [RESULT]

Greek uses the consecutive conjunction ὥστε (less often ὡς) to introduce all result clauses. In the main clauses of result constructions, the following trigger words are often found: οὕτως, "such," "thus"; τοιοῦτος, "such," "of such a kind"; τοσοῦτος, "so great."

Greek also distinguishes between real or factual results and potential or expected results. (A) Real results are expressed with the indicative mood and negated by οὐ (or one of its compounds). (B) When the result is expected or anticipated or even reflects a general tendency, the infinitive is used;[1] the infinitive is typically negated with a μή (except in an indirect statement where

1. Remember that when the subject of the infinitive differs from the subject of the main clause, a subjective accusative is used; see §4.3.4 and §12.

an οὐ is used with the infinitive only if the infinitive would have been a finite verb in direct statement). (C) When the potentiality of the result is being emphasized, the particle ἄν can be used with the infinitive, which here will be negated with μή.

(A.1) τὸ θέατρόν ἐστι τοσοῦτον ὥστε πᾶς ὁ δῆμος δύναται καθίζειν ἔνθα.

The theater is so great that all the people are able sit there. [REAL]

(B.1) τὸ θέατρόν ἐστι τοσοῦτον ὥστε πάντα τὸν δῆμον δύνασθαι καθίζειν ἔνθα.

The theater is so great that all the people should be able to sit there. [EXPECTED]

(A.2) τὸ θέατρόν ἐστι τοιοῦτον ὥστε πᾶς ὁ δῆμος οὐ δύναται καθίζειν ἔνθα.

The theater is such that all the people can't sit there. [REAL]

(B.2) τὸ θέατρόν ἐστι τοιοῦτον ὥστε πάντα τὸν δῆμον μὴ δύνασθαι καθίζειν ἔνθα.

The theater is such that all the people wouldn't be able to sit there. [EXPECTED]

(A.3) φησί τὸ θέατρον εἶναι τοιοῦτον ὥστε πάντα τὸν δῆμον οὐ δύνασθαι καθίζειν ἔνθα.

He says that the theater is such that all the people can't sit there. [REAL in Indirect Statement]

(B.3) φησί τὸ θέατρον εἶναι τοιοῦτον ὥστε πάντα τὸν δῆμον μὴ δύνασθαι καθίζειν ἔνθα.

He says that the theater is such that all the people wouldn't be able to sit there. [EXPECTED in Indirect Statement]

(C) τὸ θέατρόν ἐστι τοσοῦτον ὥστε πάντα τὸν δῆμον ἂν δύνασθαι καθίζειν ἔνθα.

The theater is so great that all the people probably should be able to sit there. [POTENTIAL]

22. OBJECT CLAUSES

So far, we have seen that some verbs can employ a noun (the direct object) to complete their meaning, and others a non-finite verb phrase containing either an infinitive or a participle. For certain types of verbs it is a subordinate clause that plays this role, appropriately called an **object clause**.

In English, these clauses are generally introduced by the conjunction "that":

I fear that the worst will happen.

Take care that the children come to no harm.

They saw to it that the people learned the truth.

An alternative conjunction, the archaic "lest," can be substituted in some contexts:

I fear lest the worst happen.

Take care lest the children come to harm.

Notice that in some instances the conjunction "that" can be eliminated, as in the first sentence above.

In Greek, there are two classes of verbs that govern object clauses:

22.1 VERBS OF EFFORT

This category includes verbs like πράττω ("bring it about that," "make sure [that]"), ἐπιμελέομαι ("take care that"), ὁράω ("see to it that"), μηχανάομαι ("contrive that"), and the like. The object clauses are usually introduced by ὅπως, and the subordinate verb is most commonly in the future indicative, in both primary and secondary sequences. The negative is ὅπως μή.

πράττε ὅπως ὁ βασιλεὺς τὴν ἐπιστολὴν ταύτην δέξεται.
Make sure that the king receives this letter.

ὁ Ὀδυσσεὺς ἐμηχανήσατο ὅπως οἱ μνηστῆρες μηδὲν ὑποπτεύσουσιν.
Odysseus contrived that the suitors would suspect nothing.

An imperative main verb can sometimes be omitted:

> ἐπιμελοῦ ὅπως μὴ ἐγερεῖς τοὺς φύλακας. → ὅπως μὴ ἐγερεῖς τοὺς φύλακας.
>
> Take care that you don't wake the guards.

22.2 VERBS OF FEARING

If the event or circumstance feared is in the future, the object clause's verb will be in the subjunctive in primary sequence and in the optative in secondary sequence (but occasionally the subjunctive here as well). The conjunction is μή when the fear is that something *will* happen, and μὴ οὐ when the fear is that it *will not* happen:

> φοβοῦμαι μὴ ὁ ἀλώπηξ τὰς ἀλεκτρυόνας φάγῃ.
>
> I fear that the fox will eat the chickens. (or: lest the fox eat the chickens)

> ἔδεισαν μὴ οἱ νεανίαι οὐ ἕλοιεν (or ἕλωσι) τὸν ἀλώπεκα.
>
> They feared that the young men would not capture the fox.

If the fear is about something in the present or past, the indicative mood is used:

> φοβοῦμαι μὴ ὁ στρατὸς νενίκηται.
>
> I fear that the army has been defeated.

A person may be afraid to do something rather than fear that something will happen. In this case, the verb of fearing will take a complementary infinitive:

> μὴ φοβήθῃς λέγειν τὴν ἀλήθειαν.
>
> Don't be afraid to tell the truth.

23. CAUSAL CLAUSES

A **causal clause** is a subordinate clause which answers the question "why?" the main clause occurred. In English, subordinate clauses are typically introduced by the conjunctions "since," "because," and "as."

Because Alexander has died, the empire is in confusion.

We will head to the agora now since an assembly will be convened soon.

As I'm not feeling very well, I'm going to bed.

In Greek, causal clauses are introduced by the conjunctions ὅτι, διότι, διόπερ, ἐπεί, ἐπειδή, or ὡς. These clauses are negated with οὐ (or one of its compounds).

Causal clauses in Greek are of four types: factual, alleged or assumed, contrafactual, or potential.

Factual clauses, whether primary or secondary, are always put in the indicative:

I help because you are in danger.
βοηθῶ διότι κινδυνεύετε.

I helped because you were in danger.
ἐβοήθησα διότι ἐκινδυνεύετε.

Alleged or assumed causals in secondary sequence are placed in the optative mood, as if there had been an implied indirect statement.

He helped because you were in danger [allegedly, or so he thought].
ἐβοήθησε ὡς κινδυνεύοιτε.

Contrafactual causals use the indicative mood with the particle ἄν.

Since you could have been in danger [but weren't], he helped.
ἐπειδὴ ἂν ἐκινδυνεύσατε, ἐβοήθησεν.

Potential causals are put in the optative with the particle ἄν.

Since you might have been in danger, he helped.
ἐπεὶ ἂν κινδυνεύσαιτε, ἐβοήθησεν.

Two alternate methods for expressing causals are quite common. As we've seen in §13, participles (whether in an absolute or not) frequently are used causally. Moreover, an articular infinitive (see §12) in the accusative after the preposition διά expresses causation.

ὑμῶν κινδυνευόντων, ἐβοήθησεν.

διὰ τὸ ὑμᾶς κινδυνεύειν, ἐβοήθησεν.

Because of your being in danger, he helped.

24. TEMPORAL CLAUSES

From a practical standpoint, defining time with some specificity is one of the most important tasks a language must perform: what happens when, what occurs before what, what transpires after what, and what things take place roughly at the same time. The importance of time has already been observed for prepositions, adverbs, conjunctions, and the tenses of verbs. We see it, too, with participles, absolute phrases, conditionals, and indirect statement. An inference can be drawn here: language recognizes a great need for pinpointing time, especially when one event takes place in a context with one or more other events.

In this chapter, we examine **temporal clauses**; that is, subordinate clauses within complex sentences, where the relationship between the main clauses and the dependent clauses is established by means of a time referent. This time referent is usually a subordinating conjunction (see §28.2) which specifies whether the action of the dependent clause is prior to, subsequent to, or roughly simultaneous with the action of the main clause.

> <u>Before email was invented</u>, there were only the telephone and letters. [SUBSEQUENT]
>
> I will hold this memory dear <u>until the day I die</u>. [SUBSEQUENT]
>
> <u>After we left</u>, the hurricane hit. [PRIOR]
>
> The hurricane hit <u>as soon as we left</u>. [PRIOR]
>
> <u>Ever since they won</u>, they've been really arrogant. [PRIOR]
>
> <u>When you arrive</u>, it will be my birthday. [SIMULTANEOUS]
>
> I sacrificed to the gods <u>so long as I was successful</u>. [SIMULTANEOUS]
>
> <u>While we were sleeping</u>, the enemy attacked. [SIMULTANEOUS]

For temporal clauses, English relies semantically more on the subordinating conjunctions than on the tenses of its verbs:

I will wait to do this until you leave.

I will wait to do this until you have left.

I will wait to do this until you will have left.

Notice how there really isn't a significant difference in meaning between these three sentences, despite the change in tense in the subordinate clauses.

In Greek, too, there's a considerable importance given to the subordinating conjunctions, but probably the most crucial feature for Greek temporal clauses is whether they're definite or indefinite. A **definite temporal clause** describes an action occurring at a definite or specific point in time. An **indefinite temporal clause** describes an action occurring A) in the indefinite or unspecified future, B) repetitively an indefinite or unspecified number of times, or, more rarely, C) continually over an indefinite or unspecified span of time. Definite temporal clauses most commonly describe actions taking place in the present or the past time; indefinite temporal clauses usually describe actions taking place in the future or else in a general past or present.

Definite temporal clauses in Greek use the indicative mood. Indefinite temporal clauses use the subjunctive mood (typically with the particle ἄν or its compounds; see §16 n.2) if there is more vividness, the optative mood (typically without the particle ἄν) if there is less vividness,[1] or the indicative mood (quite uncommon). Predictably, the negation for definite temporal clauses is οὐ (or its compounds), while for indefinite temporal clauses the negation is usually μή (or its compounds).

It was night when he came.
ἦν νὺξ ὅτε ἦλθεν.

After he came, we sacrificed.
ἐπειδὴ ἦλθεν, ἐθύσαμεν θυσίας.

We did this until he came.
ἐποιοῦμεν τοῦτο μέχρι ἦλθεν.

1. We first met the concept of vividness with conditional sentences (§17), where we defined it as more or less likely to become a reality. Thus, indefinite temporal clauses with the subjunctive can be said to be more likely to occur than indefinite temporal clauses with the optative.

We do this until he comes.

ποιοῦμεν τοῦτο μέχρι ἔλθῃ ἄν.

We do this until he should come.

ποιοῦμεν τοῦτο μέχρι ἔλθοι.

When indefinite temporal clauses describe a general action as introduced by a main verb in a primary tense (i.e., present, future, perfect, future perfect), the subjunctive with the particle ἄν (or one of its compounds) is used; but if the general action is introduced by a main verb in a secondary tense (i.e., imperfect, aorist, pluperfect), the optative is used.

It was night whenever he came.

ἦν νὺξ ὅτε ἔλθοι.

Whenever he comes, we sacrifice.

ὅταν ἔλθῃ θύομεν θυσίας.

We did this until he was to come.

ἐποιοῦμεν τοῦτο ἕως ἔλθοι.

We do this until he is to come.

ποιοῦμεν τοῦτο ἕως ἂν ἔλθῃ.

24.1 CONSTRUCTIONS WITH πρίν

The only anomaly to the foregoing is offered by the temporal conjunction πρίν ("until," "before"), which is accompanied by its own specific syntax.

(1) When a main clause is negated and a definite temporal clause in the past introduced by πρίν is used, the subordinate clause is usually in the indicative mood.

He does not come until we have ordered.

οὐκ ἔρχεται πρὶν κεκελεύκαμεν.

(2) When a main clause in the future or general past or present is negated <u>and</u> an indefinite temporal clause in the present or future introduced by πρίν is used, the subordinate clause is usually in the subjunctive mood with ἄν.

He will not come until we order.

οὐκ εἶσι <u>πρὶν κελεύωμεν ἄν</u>.

(3) Finally, when a main clause is not negated and thus has less of a contingent quality (or even if it is negated but has absolutely no contingent quality), πρίν introduces a purely temporal clause in which the infinitive is used.

He comes before we order.

ἔρχεται <u>πρὶν</u> ἡμᾶς <u>κελεύειν</u>.

As you have probably noted from several of the sentences in this chapter, temporal clauses often have a contingent quality recalling conditional sentences; they also have, moreover, some overlap with purpose clauses and relative clauses, which are treated in §§20 and 19, respectively.

You may find it helpful to study temporal clauses if they're presented in tabular form:

TYPE	TIME	MAIN CLAUSE	TEMPORAL CLAUSE	NEGATION
Definite	Present	Indicative[2]	Indicative	οὐ[3]
	Past			
	Future[1]			
Indefinite	Primary General	present, future, perfect or fut. perfect Indicative[2]	Subjunctive with ἄν[3]	μή[3]
	Secondary General	imperfect, aorist, or pluperfect Indicative[2]	Optative	μή[3]
	Future More Vivid	Indicative[2]	Subjunctive with ἄν[3]	μή[3]
	Future Less Vivid	Indicative[2]	Optative	μή[3]
πρίν *not* negated Definite	Present	Indicative[2]	Infinitive	οὐ[3]
	Past			
	Future			
πρίν negated Definite	Present	Indicative[2]	Indicative	οὐ[3]
	Past			
πρίν negated Indefinite/ General	Present	Indicative[2]	Subjunctive with ἄν	μή[3]
	Past			
	Future			

1. Extremely rare.
2. Unless ambient grammar requires otherwise.
3. Or one of its compounds (see §11.6).

25. INTERROGATIVE SENTENCES

Any English declarative sentence can be turned into a question with no syntactic alteration. In speaking, such a sentence is marked as interrogative by a rising voice inflection at the end; in writing, this is accomplished by a change in punctuation:

Socrates is the wisest man in Athens.

Socrates is the wisest man in Athens?

Most commonly however, the change from a declarative to an interrogative sentence is marked by slight changes in syntax. If the main verb of the sentence is a form of the verb "to be," interrogation is indicated by a reverse in word order of the subject and verb.

Socrates is the wisest man in Athens.

Is Socrates the wisest man in Athens?

Similarly, in a sentence with a verb augmented with an auxiliary, the order of the subject and the auxiliary verb is reversed:

Socrates has been put to death.

Has Socrates been put to death?

Finally, sentences with simple verbs are turned into questions through the use of the auxiliary verb "do":

The Athenians admire(d) wise men.

Do the Athenians admire wise men?

Did the Athenians admire wise men?

Questions that ask for other types of information besides yes-or-no answers are introduced by interrogative pronouns and adverbs, placed at the beginning of the sentence. Interrogative pronouns are used exactly as personal pronouns would be:

The Athenians executed Socrates.

Who executed Socrates?

Questions introduced by interrogative adverbs involve the word-order changes listed above:

Why is Socrates the wisest man in Athens?

Where has Socrates been put to death?

How much do the Athenians admire wise men?

Yes-or-no questions can be asked in such a way as to indicate that the speaker expects a particular answer:

You are going to the festival, aren't you?

You are not going to wear that, are you?

In Greek, the situation is actually less complex. Interrogative pronouns, adjectives, and adverbs are regularly placed at or near the beginning of the sentence, just as in English:

τίς τοῦτό σοι εἶπεν;
Who told you this?

ποῖ ἐληλύθασι πάντες οἱ φιλόσοφοι;
Where have all the philosophers gone?

Yes-or-no questions are commonly (but not necessarily) introduced with the interrogative particle ἆρα:

ἆρα φιλεῖς ἐκείνην τὴν γυναῖκα;
Do you love that woman?

Greek also allows the questioner to prejudice the answer, either as positive (with the particles οὐ, ἆρ' οὐ, or οὐκοῦν), or in the negative (with μή, ἆρα μή, or μῶν):

ἆρ' οὐ φιλεῖς ἐκείνην τὴν γυναῖκα;
Don't you love that woman?

μῶν φιλεῖς ἐκείνην τὴν γυναῖκα;
You don't love that woman, do you?

IV. SOME OTHER GRAMMATICAL ELEMENTS

26. ADVERBS

Adverbs have traditionally been defined as words which specifically modify adjectives, verbs, and other adverbs:

We gladly listened to Socrates. [MODIFYING A VERB]

This play is deservedly famous. [MODIFYING AN ADJECTIVE]

They fought uncharacteristically poorly. [MODIFYING AN ADVERB]

In modern English usage, adverbs can commonly be seen to modify entire clauses or sentences:

Sadly, Mr. Smith passed away yesterday.

Hopefully, it will rain tomorrow.

Regrettably, no one showed up.

Interestingly, they're all Canadians.

Embarrassingly, the chairs were already taken.

Supposedly, they're coming today.

These "sentence adverbs" are typically placed first in their clause; if placed last in their clause, they come off as an apparent afterthought:

It will rain tomorrow, hopefully.

All the chairs were already taken, embarrassingly.

They're coming today, supposedly.

Most English adverbs express temporal or locative relations, manner, or degree:

You will arrive later. [TEMPORAL]

The people worship no gods there. [LOCATIVE]

They easily won. [MANNER]

This amount is far greater. [DEGREE]

An interesting feature of English usage, the use of adjectives with pronouns in the subjective case is sometimes felt to be awkward and is therefore replaced with the use of an adverb:

I, happy, went on my way.

Happy, I went on my way.

Happily, I went on my way.

This replacement in the objective case is not so simple:

He gave the book to happy me.

He gave the book to me, happy.

These two sentences seem quite awkward, but no adverbial replacement is available. Hence, some sort of grammatical expansion must be employed:

He gave the book to me, and I was happy.

He gave the book to me, making me happy.

He gave the book to me, for which I was happy.

The functions and usage of the Greek adverb are comparable to the English.

Σωκράτους ἡδέως ἠκούομεν.
We gladly listened to Socrates.

τοῦτο τὸ δρᾶμα ἀξίως εὐδόκιμον.
This play is deservedly famous.

ἐπολέμισαν καινῶς κακῶς.
They fought uncharacteristically poorly.

ἀφίξεσθε ὕστερον.

You will arrive later.

τὸ ἦθος ἐνταῦθα σεβῶνται θεοὺς οὔτινας.

The people worship no gods there.

ῥᾳδίως ἐνίκησαν.

They easily won.

οὗτος ὁ ἄριθμός ἐστι πολλῷ πλείων.

This amount is far greater.

26.1 FINE POINTS

Now that you've graduated from Greek Adverbs 101, let's look at some of the finer points of this part of speech in Greek.

First, one could appropriately say that many of the Greek particles (see §27) serve as the structural and functional equivalents of sentence adverbs.

The Greek adverb, when found in the attributive position, can form part of a noun phrase (see §7):

οἱ ἔνδον ἐκάλεσαν τοὺς ἐκτός.

The ones inside called to the ones outside.

Though somewhat rare, an adverb can be used with a substantive whose deverbative force is being emphasized:[1]

μάλα στρατηγός (< στρατηγεῖν)

an excellent general, really a general, much the general, generalissimo

Some locative and temporal adverbs are used with the genitive of separation (and other genitives) and thus function as prepositions:

ἄνευ ἐκείνων: without those

1. This usage probably evolved out of the use of adverbs with other deverbative nouns, like infinitives and verbals:

μάλα στρατηγεῖν: to really general, to general greatly

μάλα στρατηγητέον: it really must be generalled, it greatly needs generalling ἔξω τούτου: out of this

χωρὶς δούλων: without slaves

You should notice how many parts of speech can be translated adverbially into English:

prepositional phrases:

μετὰ τῶν νόμων: according to the laws → legally

κατὰ τὴν πόλιν: throughout the city → citywide

substantives in the dative or accusative:

θυμῷ: with passion → passionately

πάντα: in all respects → utterly

participial phrases:

ὢν εὐδαίμων: being lucky → luckily

adjectival phrases:

παντελὴς καὶ δικαῖος: perfect and just → perfectly just

26.2 DEGREES OF COMPARISON

Like adjectives (see §6.2), many adverbs have three **degrees of comparison**: positive, comparative, and superlative. The most common endings for positive adverbs are -ῶς and -έως (like English "-ly"); for comparatives, -τερον, -ιον, and -ον (English "more ______ly," "rather ______ly"); and for superlatives -(εσ)τατα and -ιστα (English "most ______ly," "very ______ly").

Like English, some very common Greek adverbs exhibit irregular comparatives and superlatives built on different stems. As you will encounter these words often, it will be helpful to you to master them:

well (capably, excellently): εὖ, ἀμεῖνον, ἄριστα

well (virtuously): εὖ, or rarely ἀγαθῶς, βελτίον, βέλτιστα

well (strongly): εὖ,κρεῖττον, κράτιστα

well (beautifully): καλῶς, κάλλιον, κάλλιστα

badly, ill, poorly: κακῶς, κακίον, κάκιστα

badly, ill, poorly: κακῶς, χεῖρον, [no superlative]

greatly, mightily: μέγα or μεγάλως or μεγάλα, μεῖζον, μέγιστον

slightly, a little: μικροῦ or μικρόν, ἔλαττον, ἐλάχιστα or ἐλάχιστον

much: μάλα, μᾶλλον, μάλιστα

much: πολύ or πολλά, πλέον or πλεῖν, πλεῖστα or πλεῖστον

rarely, scantily: ὀλίγου, [no comparative], ὀλιγίστου

soon: τάχα, θᾶττον, τάχιστα

swiftly: ταχέως, θᾶττον, τάχιστα

Some common irregular adverbs which lack positive degrees are:

badly, ill, poorly: ἧττον, ἥκιστα

less: μεῖον, [no superlative]

before, prior: πρότερον, πρῶτα or πρῶτον

after, later: ὕστερον or ὕστερα, ὕστατα or ὕστατον

27. PARTICLES

Particles, as we defined in §2.7, are little words (or non-words) which are added to a clause or sentence to contribute some nuance or cue that aids in the interpretation of that sentence or clause. For example,

I hate this game.

Arrgh, I hate this game.

In the first of these sentences, the listener or reader won't necessarily know why the speaker hates the game. In the second sentence, the presence of "arrgh" communicates to the listener or reader that the speaker hates the game due to some frustration.

One way in which you can distinguish between a particle and an interjection is word position: generally, an interjection can be placed anywhere in its sentence or clause, while a particle can usually be placed in only one or two positions within its context:

Arrgh, I hate this game.

Or,

I hate this game, arrgh.

But not:

I hate, arrgh, this game.

As we saw in the previous chapter, particles and sentence adverbs bear some functional similarities, as do sentence conjunctions and particles (see the next chapter).

The most important thing to note about Greek particles is their virtual ubiquity in all genres of literature. Placed, typically, as either the first or second word of their clause,[1] they serve as a constant signal to readers how to interpret that clause. Because particles can be used in common combinations, one can find clauses or sentences where the first three or four words are all particles. In translation, readers will sometimes opt not to translate a given particle, but

1. When a particle isn't customarily found as the first word of its sentence or clause, it is referred to as **postpositive**.

they should *never* ignore the tone, coloration, or nuance that particles lend to the Greek language.

Too numerous to list here, particles should be mastered with a special diligence, precisely because they are much more important to Greek stylistics than they are to English.

28. CONJUNCTIONS

As we saw in §2.8, **conjunctions** are words that link grammatically equivalent words, phrases, clauses, or even sentences. There are two general types of conjunction:

28.1 COORDINATING

Coordinating conjunctions link words, phrases, clauses, and sentences, like for like:

words: sings and dances

phrases: in the ballpark but out of fair territory

clauses: we don't swim nor do they sail

sentences: I quit the job. For I am weary and frustrated.[1]

Correlatives are a common type of coordinating conjunctions, where one correlative is found in each coordinate clause or phrase. The most common correlatives are: "both . . . and," "either . . . or," "neither . . . nor," "not only . . . but also," and "on the one hand . . . on the other (hand)."

28.2 SUBORDINATING

Subordinating conjunctions operate solely on the level of linking clauses: specifically, a main clause and a subordinate clause (see §3.2):

I will read the book, when you finish it.
[MAIN CLAUSE] [SUBORDINATE CLAUSE]

Just as my mother taught me, I always speak the truth.
[SUBORDINATE CLAUSE] [MAIN CLAUSE]

1. Starting about the mid-20th century, formal American English began to frown on the use of most sentence conjunctions; Greek, on the other hand, is especially fond of them.

In English, there is a much wider array of subordinating conjunctions than coordinating conjunctions, despite the fact that the latter are used in a greater variety of settings.

So too, in Greek, coordinating conjunctions are probably more frequent and widespread, while subordinating conjunctions are more specific in meaning and more numerous in variety. The most common coordinating (and correlative) conjunctions according to type are:

DISJUNCTIVE: ἤ, "or"; ἤ . . . ἤ, "either . . . or"; εἶτε . . . εἶτε, "either . . . or"

ADVERSATIVE: ἀλλά, δέ, ἀτάρ, μέντοι, καίτοι, "but," "yet," "however," "and yet," "but yet"

COPULATIVE: καί, τέ, "and"; τέ . . . τέ, τέ . . . καί, καί . . . καί, "both . . . and"; οὐδέ (μηδέ) . . . οὐδέ (μηδέ), οὔτε (μήτε) . . . οὔτε (μήτε), "neither . . . nor"[2]

CAUSAL: γάρ, "for"

CONSEQUENTIAL: ἄρα, νῦν, οὖν, "then," "therefore," "accordingly"; τοίνυν, τοιγάρτοι, τοιγαροῦν, "so then," "now then," "so therefore"

ἢ κατὰ τὴν γῆν ἢ κατὰ τὴν θάλατταν

either by land or by sea

δικαῖος ἀλλὰ πικρός

just but harsh

οὔτε ἐν τῇ πόλει οὔτε ἐν τῷ ἀγρῷ

neither in the city nor in the country

ἑτοῖμός ἐστι, νέος γάρ ἐστιν.

He is ready, for he is young.

φρονῶ· ὑπάρχω τοιγαροῦν.

I think; therefore I am.

Some coordinating conjunctions, when they link sentences or clauses, can serve as particles (see §27).

2. See §11.6 for the contexts where μήτε and μηδέ would replace οὔτε and οὐδέ.

The Greek subordinating conjunctions are far too numerous to list. Some are exclusively subordinating; others can also be used in coordination. They can be classified into the following taxonomy:

TEMPORAL (see §24): conjunctions meaning "when," "before," "after," "between," "until," etc.

CAUSAL (see §23): conjunctions meaning "since," "because," etc.

CONCESSIVE (see §18): conjunctions meaning "though," "although," "even though," "even if," etc.

COMPARATIVE: conjunctions meaning "as" (ὡς, ὅπως), "just as" (ὥσπερ), "according as" (καθάπερ), etc.

CONDITIONAL (see §17): conjunctions meaning "if," "provided that," "so long as," etc.

FINAL and CONSECUTIVE (see §20 and §21): conjunctions meaning "so that," "in order that," "such that," "so as to," "that," "to," etc.

LOCATIVE: conjunctions meaning "where," "at which" (οὗ, ὅπου); "whence," "from which" (ὅθεν, ὁπόθεν); "whither," "to which" (οἷ, ὅποι); etc.

RELATIVE (see §19): pronominal conjunctions meaning "who," "which," "whom," "whose," "of which," "to whom," "to which," etc.

Relative conjunctions and some locative conjunctions also function as pronouns. Some of the other Greek subordinating conjunctions also serve as adverbs, especially sentence adverbs (see §26).

29. INTERJECTIONS

As noted in §2.9, **interjections** are grammatically and syntactically very loose elements which can be added to clauses or sentences to convey elevated emotions or emphasis.

The most notable feature of interjections in English is their potential placement in almost any position within a sentence or clause:

> Dammit all, I wish that this day would end.
>
> I wish, dammit all, that this day would end.
>
> I wish that this day, dammit all, would end.
>
> I wish that this day would end, dammit all.

Because Greek survives to us primarily as a literary language, and because interjections are found primarily in colloquial usage, we know relatively few Greek interjections. Due to its frequency in tragedy, the most familiar is οἴμοι "alas," but a few others are worth noting: εὖγε "yay!" "hooray!"; αἰβοί "yuck!" "uggh!"; ἰοῦ "oh!" "alas!"; εἶεν "okay!" "great!"; ἢ ἤ "tsk tsk!" "tut tut!"; φεῦ "alas"; φέρε and ἄγε "c'mon!"[1]

1. The last two, φέρε and ἄγε, were originally singular imperatives, but their use became so common that their origins were forgotten or ignored, and they began to be used even in grammatically plural contexts.

INDEX OF TERMS

See also the table of contents. A bolded number indicates the page where a definition for the term is provided.